STUDY GUIDE TO ACCOMPANY

TORT LAW FOR LEGAL ASSISTANTS

LINDA L. EDWARDS, J.D., Professor
Phoenix College

J. STANLEY EDWARDS, J.D., Adjunct Professor
Phoenix College

WEST PUBLISHING COMPANY
Minneapolis/St. Paul New York Los Angeles San Francisco

WEST'S COMMITMENT TO THE ENVIRONMENT

In 1906, West Publishing Company began recycling materials left over from the production of books. This began a tradition of efficient and responsible use of resources. Today, up to 95% of our legal books and 70% of our college texts are printed on recycled, acid-free stock. West also recycles nearly 22 million pounds of scrap paper annually—the equivalent of 181,717 trees. Since the 1960s, West has devised ways to capture and recycle waste inks, solvents, oils, and vapors created in the printing process. We also recycle plastics of all kinds, wood, glass, corrugated cardboard, and batteries, and have eliminated the use of styrofoam book packaging. We at West are proud of the longevity and the scope of our commitment to our environment.

Production, Prepress, Printing and Binding by West Publishing Company.

610 Opperman Drive
P.O. Box 64526
St. Paul, MN 55164–0526

Printed in the United States of America
99 98 97 96 95 94 93 92 8 7 6 5 4 3 2 1 0

ISBN 0–314–00696–6

INTRODUCTION

Time management is probably one of the most serious problems college students must confront today. Most are employed at least part-time and have family and civic duties as well. Therefore, minimal time devoted to study and "taking the path of least resistance", which frequently entails reading material once or twice prior to an exam, is often tempting.

Unfortunately, research relating to the learning process shows the mere act of reading to be a highly inefficient and often unprofitable way of studying. Characteristic statements of those who have not really learned what they have read is "I knew the material until I took the exam and then my mind went blank" or "I understand what I read; I just can't take tests." Serious self-examination in most instances would reveal that the "understanding" of the material was superficial. The student might, for example, be able to recognize the correct answers (as in the form of a multiple choice exam) but might not be able to restate the information in his/her own words or to apply the information in an actual situation.

Those students who perform best in school are those who find some way of becoming actively engaged in the learning process. Writing, whether it be in the form of notetaking, preparing summaries or developing outlines, is one way of becoming actively involved. The purpose of the study guides that follow is to take you beyond passively reading over the content of the text and require you to consciously work with the material presented.

You can use the study guides in one of two ways. You may read a chapter all the way through once, highlighting material you think is important or writing notes in the margins, and then attempting to answer the study guide questions. Alternatively, you may want to refer to the study guide as you read through a chapter to help you focus on key ideas and to insure that you are staying actively engaged while you read.

Notice that each study guide question is followed by a number in parentheses. This number refers to the page number(s) on which the answer to the study guide question can be found.

You may be tempted to postpone answering the study guide questions until immediately before the exam or you may try to answer them in your head without committing the answers to paper. Remember, however, that the purpose of these study guides is to shift you from being one who passively reads material to one who actively participates in the learning process. You compromise that purpose when you take shortcuts.

One caveat in using the study guides - do not assume that

simply because you can find the answer to a question in the study guide that you necessarily understand that answer. In other words, you may be able to match the appropriate phrase or sentence in the text to a particular question but you may have not have a clear idea of what that phrase or sentence means. In those instances ask your instructor to give you an alternative explanation or provide you with some concrete examples for clarification.

Samples of legal documents, forms and discovery materials are included in the study guides. These materials are illustrative of the types of documents and forms you will encounter in a law office setting. Therefore, you might enjoy perusing them to familiarize yourself with their general format and content. As much as possible, the samples relate to the discussion in the Practice Pointers section of the corresponding chapter. In some chapters such correlation was impossible or impracticable, in which case the sample was chosen because of its significance to tort law practice and not because of any particular correspondence to the information presented in that chapter.

Use the study guides in the spirit in which they are intended and you will enhance your chances of being a successful student and practitioner. Good luck in your exploration of the fascinating realm of tort law. May these study guides provide you with the keys you need to open the doors to understanding!

TABLE OF CONTENTS

STUDY GUIDE
CHAPTER ONE

1. What is one of the arguments regarding risk allocation in reference to tort law? (4)

(a) What is the counterargument that could be raised in opposition to that argument? (4)

2. What is one definition of a tort? (4)

3. What are the three categories of torts? (4)

(a)

(b)

(c)

4. What are the problems inherent in proving the reasonableness of one's conduct? (5)

5. Under what circumstances is reasonableness of conduct not relevant? (5)

6. What ideals dominate any public policy discussion regarding tort law? (6)

7. For what reason do some argue that societal interests need to be considered even when mediating disputes between individuals? (6)

(a) Why do others argue that society should have minimal impact on disputes between individuals? (6)

8. What is the relationship between morality and tort law? (6)

9. What is a slippery slope argument? (7)

(a) Give an example of such an argument. (7)

(b) In what way are the courts influenced by slippery slope arguments? (7)

10. From what sources is tort law derived? (7)

(a) What is the Restatement and how is it used? (7-8)

11. What are four differences between torts and crimes? (8-9)

(a)

(b)

(c)

(d)

12. What are two differences between torts and contracts? (9)
(a)

(b)

13. What was the role of the blood feud in barbaric societies? (10)

(a) What alternative to the blood feud was developed in early Anglo-Saxon history? (10)

14. What is an action in trespass? (11)

(a) What has to be proved? (11)

15. What is a trespass on the case? (12)

(a) How does it differ from an action in trespass? (13)

16. What is the status of the action in trespass and trespass on the case today? (13)

17. What effect did the development of public transportation have on tort law? (13)

18. In what sense have we come full circle in tort law? (13)

REVIEW QUESTIONS

1. Who do you think should bear the responsibility for injuries caused if no one is at fault for those injuries? What is the basis for your opinion?

(a) Who do you think should be responsible if both the victim and the person responsible for the victim's injuries are both partially at fault? Why?

2. What factors are taken into consideration in deciding whether an individual should be held liable for his actions?

3. How does the purpose of tort law differ from criminal law? From contract law?

4. Describe the evolution of tort law.

PUTTING IT INTO PRACTICE

Suppose that a friend of yours is complaining about a case she read about in which someone sued a cigarette manufacturer after contracting cancer. Your friend argues that pretty soon everyone who is hurt will be able to make someone pay for his/her injuries. Explain to your friend the reasoning behind holding manufacturers strictly liable. Include a brief description of how tort law has changed over time. Explain also why some people are in agreement with her and tell her why the argument she is using is characterized as a slippery slope argument.

KEY TERMS

Define the following:

Action in trespass

Public policy

Slippery slope argument

Trespass on the case

The following page is an example of a simple retainer agreement. Your state may require a more sophisticated agreement setting forth all of the attorney's potential responsibilities.

RETAINER AGREEMENT

Agreement dated this 3rd day of January, 1992, by and between SUSAN SMITH and J. Stanley Edwards, EDWARDS & EDWARDS, Attorneys at Law.

1. I do hereby employ J. Stanley Edwards to represent me and my interests in any and all matters and/or causes of action that I may have arising out of an accident in which I was involved on December 26, 1991.

2. I hereby agree that the attorney's fees are to be based upon a contingency fee basis of thirty-three and one-third percent (33⅓%) of the gross recovery received. It is my understanding that there will be no attorney's fees if no sums are recovered. I hereby further agree to be responsible for all out-of-pocket expenses arising out of any action taken in this matter and that no settlement shall be made without my consent.

____
Susan Smith

EDWARDS & EDWARDS

By ________________________________
J. Stanley Edwards
For the Firm

STUDY GUIDE
CHAPTER TWO

1. What is the purpose of a demand letter? (18)

2. What are the four basic elements of a complaint? (19)

   (a)

   (b)

   (c)

   (d)

3. How much factual detail is required in a complaint? (19)

4. What is a verification? (19)

   (a) Must a verification always be submitted? (19)

5. In what circumstance would it be appropriate for a party to file a default judgment? (19)

6. What are five things a defendant can do in response to a complaint? (19-20)

(a)

(b)

(c)

(d)

(e)

7. Who has the burden of proving an affirmative defense? (20)

8. What is the difference between a counterclaim and a crossclaim? (20)

9. What is a defendant asserting when she files a motion for failure to state a claim upon which relief can be granted? (20)

(a) What is the relationship between this motion and a demurrer? (20)

10. What is the theory underlying discovery? (20)

(a) What is the significance of the discovery process? (20)

11. What is the difference between interrogatories and depositions? (21)

(a) In what circumstance might an attorney prefer interrogatories to a deposition? (21)

(b) In what circumstance might an attorney prefer a deposition to interrogatories? (21)

12. What is the purpose of sending out requests for admissions? (21)

(a) What are the consequences of failing to respond to a request for admissions? (21)

13. What is the purpose of a request for production of documents? (21)

14. What is the purpose underlying a request for medical examination? (21)

15. What is the difference between a motion to compel and a motion for a protective order? (21-22)

16. When is it appropriate to file a motion for summary judgment? (22)

(a) How is a motion for summary judgment rebutted? (22)

17. What is the purpose of a pretrial conference? (22)

18. At what point and for what purpose would an attorney make a motion in limine? (22)

19. What is a bench trial? (22)

20. What is the purpose of <u>voir dire?</u> (23)

21. What is the difference between a challenge for cause and a peremptory challenge? (23)

(a) Is there any limit put on the number of such challenges an attorney can raise? (23)

22. What does an attorney attempt to do during opening statements? (23)

(a) Of what importance to jurors are opening statements? (23)

23. What burden of proof does the plaintiff in a tort case bear? (23)

24. What is the purpose of cross-examination? (23)

25. At what point and for what reason might an attorney move for a directed verdict? (23-24)

(a) What is the result if such a motion is granted? (23)

26. What does an attorney attempt to do during closing arguments? (24)

27. What is the purpose of charging the jury? (24)

(a) Why do attorneys put so much emphasis on jury instructions? (24)

28. What is the difference between a general verdict and a special verdict?

29. What is the difference between a motion for a new trial and a motion for a judgment notwithstanding the verdict (JNOV)? (24)

(a) What conditions must be met before such motions can be made? (24)

30. If an issue is res judicata, what does that mean? (24)

REVIEW QUESTIONS

1. Make a list of all the tools that can be used for discovery.

2. Review the four elements of a complaint and establish a reason justifying the need for each of these elements.

3. Make a chronological list of all of those acts that an attorney performs during the course of a trial and establish the purpose for each of those acts.

4. Identify those words in the Key Terms with which you are unfamiliar. If you have difficulty remembering any of these words, create sentences in which you use these terms. For further practice, try, without using the text, to engage someone in conversation using these terms. If you find this too embarrassing to do, have an imaginary conversation.

PUTTING IT INTO PRACTICE

Have another person role play the part of a new client and you play the part of a legal assistant. Explain to the client, who has been injured in an automobile accident and wants to sue, what steps your firm will have to go through prior to going to trial, during trial and possibly after trial. Be sure to explain the purpose behind each step.

KEY TERMS

Define the following:

Affirmative defense

Answer

Bench trial

Challenge for cause

Charging the jury

Complaint

Counterclaim

Crossclaim

Default judgment

Demand letter

Demurrer

Deposition

Directed verdict

Discovery

General verdict

Interrogatories

JNOV

Motion for protective order

Motion for summary judgment

Motion *in limine*

Motion to compel

Peremptory challenge

Pretrial conference

Res judicata

Request for admissions

Request for medical examination

Request for production of documents

Special verdict

Verification

Voir dire

The following pages contain a sample complaint.

J. Stanley Edwards
EDWARDS & EDWARDS
11000 North Scottsdale Road
Suite No. 135
Scottsdale, Arizona 85254
Tel: (602) 991-1938
Fax: (602) 991-2480
State Bar No. 004190

Attorneys for Plaintiff

IN THE SUPERIOR COURT OF THE STATE OF ARIZONA

IN AND FOR THE COUNTY OF MARICOPA

SONJA R. Plaintiff, vs. TAMMIE D. and JOHN DOE her husband, Defendants.	No. ____________ COMPLAINT (Tort - Motor Vehicle)

Plaintiff, by and through counsel undersigned, in support of her cause of action against the Defendants alleges as follows:

1. That Plaintiff is a resident of Maricopa County, Arizona, and the cause of action referred to herein occurred in and is payable in Maricopa County, Arizona.

2. That Defendants Tammie D. and John Doe are, upon information and belief, residents of the State of Arizona; at all relevant times hereto Defendant Tammie D. was acting on behalf of herself and her marital community; that the true name of

John Doe is unknown to Plaintiff at this time and leave of the Court is requested to substitute his true name when it becomes known to Plaintiff.

3. That on or about May 31, 1990, Defendant Tammie D. did so negligently operate her motor vehicle so as to cause a collision with the 1989 Nissan Kingcab pickup truck being driven by Plaintiff, said accident occurring at Milepost 199.7 on Arizona Interstate 17, Phoenix, Maricopa County, Arizona.

4. That as a result of the negligence of Defendant Tammie D. , Plaintiff sustained medical injuries requiring treatment; was unable to perform her occupation due to the injuries sustained in the accident and has suffered a loss of earnings and been forced to endure substantial pain and suffer.

5. That as a result of the negligence of Defendant Tammie D. , Plaintiff's vehicle sustained substantial damage.

WHEREFORE, Plaintiff demands Judgment against the Defendants, and each of them, jointly and severally, as follows:

1. For Plaintiff's general damages in an amount to be shown by the evidence;

2. For special damages in an amount to be shown by the evidence;

3. For Plaintiff's costs incurred herein; and

4. For such other and further relief as the Court deems just and equitable.

DATED this ____ day of April, 1992.

EDWARDS & EDWARDS

By ______________________________

J. Stanley Edwards
11000 North Scottsdale Road
Suite No. 135
Scottsdale, Arizona 85254
Attorneys for Plaintiff

STUDY GUIDE
CHAPTER THREE

1. What is the procedural history of a case? (32)

2. What is a case of first impression? (32)

3. Is the issue always explicitly stated in an opinion? (32)

4. What is the difference between procedural and substantive facts? (32)

5. What is a court's holding? (33)

(a) How does a holding differ from dictum? (33)

6. What is a concurring opinion and why might a judge be moved to write such an opinion? (33)

(a) If a judge disagrees with the majority, what kind of opinion does he/she write? (34)

7. What are the elements of a brief? (34)

(a)

(b)

(c)

(d)

(e)

8. What is the purpose of briefing a case? (34)

9. What facts should be included in a brief? (34)

(a) On what basis might you decide if a fact is relevant? (34)

10. What is IRAC and what does it have to do with legal analysis? (37)

11. When writing a memorandum should you discuss both sides of an issue or only the position most favorable to your client? (38)

12. When you are comparing a court opinion to the facts of your case, how should you deal with factual differences? (39)

13. What is conclusory writing and why should it be avoided? (39)

14. Can you avoid drawing a conclusion when doing legal analysis if you have insufficient facts? (39)

REVIEW QUESTIONS

1. What are the elements of a brief? What additional elements may be found in a court opinion?

2. Suppose you have found a case that involves a rule of law you would like to see adopted by the appellate court reviewing a case involving your firm's client. How will you go about analyzing the case to determine if that rule of law might be applicable?

PUTTING IT INTO PRACTICE

Practice reading and briefing the two cases (Godbehere v. Phoenix Newspapers, Inc. and VanCamp v. ICG Management Co.) included in this chapter.

KEY TERMS

Define the following:

Appellant

Binding authority

Briefing

Case of first impression

Conclusory writing

Concurring opinion

Dictum

Holding

IRAC

Persuasive authority

Procedural facts

Procedural history

Rationale

Substantive facts

Following the two cases is a sample settlement memorandum.

783 P.2d 781

Richard G. GODBEHERE; David Carter; Robert W. Malone; Jerome Ellison; Salvatore A. Dicciccio; Jerry White; David Hendershott; Steve Werner; Richard Rosky; Patricia Mann; Brian Carnahan; Thomas Shorts; Roy Reyer; Gary Godbehere; Ray Jones; Larry Wendt; Gary Freund; Cliff Anderson; James F. Porter; Paul B. Thornton; Phillip A. Babb; Ralph Pendergast; Kirby D. Moore; Kirk L. Meisner; Clark W. Chapman; Patrick C. Cooper; Robert D. Roepke; Michael R. Mitchell; Samuel M. Grimes; Dennis G. Dowell; Mark Battilana; and David Toporek, Plaintiffs/Appellants,

v.

PHOENIX NEWSPAPERS, INC.; Randy Collier; Darrow Tully; Richard Robertson; Tom Fitzpatrick; Pat Flannery; Tony Natale; Pat Murphy; Susan Leonard; Phil Sunkel; Alan Moyer; Lynne Holt; Jay Brashear; John Kolbe; and Victor Dricks, Defendants/Appellees.

No. CV–87–0379–PR.

Supreme Court of Arizona.

Oct. 26, 1989.

Reconsideration Denied Dec. 19, 1989.

Sheriffs, deputies, and civilian employees of sheriff's office brought libel and invasion of privacy action against newspapers. The Superior Court, Maricopa County, Frederick J. Martone, J., dismissed invasion of privacy claim, and plaintiffs appealed. The Court of Appeals, 155 Ariz. 389, 746 P.2d 1319, affirmed. The Supreme Court, Feldman, V.C.J., held that: (1) cause of action for false light invasion of privacy would be recognized; (2) defendant is not liable unless the publication places the plaintiff in a false light highly offensive to a reasonable person; (3) false light cause of action may arise from publication of true information which creates a false implication about the individual; (4) public official in false light action must show that defendant published with knowledge of false innuendo or with reckless disregard of the truth; and (5) plaintiff cannot sue for false light invasion of privacy if he or she is a public official and the publication relates to the performance of his or her public life or duties.

Opinion of Court of Appeals vacated, trial court's dismissal affirmed, and cause remanded.

1. Action ⇐38(4)

Fact that both intentional infliction of emotional distress and invasion of privacy addressed the same injury is not reason to refuse to recognize two separate torts to protect against different wrongful conduct.

2. Action ⇐38(4)

Fact that outrage and invasion of privacy both provide redress for emotional injury does not mean that the two actions are merged or that a plaintiff is required to prove the former in an action for the later.

3. Torts ⇐8.5(5)

Plaintiff in false light invasion of privacy case must prove that the defendant published with knowledge of the falsity or reckless disregard for the truth; standard is as stringent as the intentional infliction of emotional distress requirement that the plaintiff prove that the defendant intentionally and recklessly caused the emotional distress.

4. Torts ⇐8.5(5)

Defendant is not liable in a false light invasion of privacy case unless the publication places the plaintiff in a false light highly offensive to a reasonable person; plaintiff's subjective threshold of sensibility is not the measure, and trivial indignities are not actionable.

5. Torts ⇐8.5(5)

Tort action for false light invasion of privacy provides protection against a narrow class of wrongful conduct that falls short of outrage, but nevertheless should be deterred.

6. Libel and Slander ⇐1
Torts ⇐8.5(5)

Although both defamation and false light invasion of privacy involve publication, the nature of the interest protected by each action differs substantially.

7. Libel and Slander ⇐6(1, 2), 30, 117

Defamation action compensates damage to reputation or good name caused by publication of false information; to be defamatory, publication must be false and must bring the defamed person into disrepute, contempt, or ridicule, or must impeach plaintiff's honesty, integrity, virtue, or reputation.

8. Torts ⇐8.5(5)

False light invasion of privacy action does not protect reputation but protects mental and emotional interests.

9. Torts ⇐8.5(5)

Plaintiff may recover for false light invasion of privacy even in the absence of a reputational damage, as long as the publicity is unreasonably offensive and attributes false characteristics, but the publication must involve a major misrepresentation of plaintiff's character, history, activities, or beliefs, and not merely minor or unimportant inaccuracies.

10. Libel and Slander ⇐30, 54

To be defamatory, publication must be false, and truth is a defense.

11. Torts ⇐8.5(5)

False light invasion of privacy case may arise when something untrue has been published about an individual or when the publication of true information creates a false implication about the individual; in the latter type of case, the false innuendo created by the highly offensive representation of a true fact constitutes the injury.

12. Torts ⚷8.5(5)

Tort of false light invasion of privacy as articulated by the Restatement § 652E is recognized in Arizona.

13. Torts ⚷8.5(5)

As in defamation, public official in a false light invasion of privacy action must always show that the defendant published with knowledge of false innuendo or with reckless disregard of the truth.

14. Torts ⚷8.5(7)

There can be no false light invasion of privacy action for matter involving official acts or duties of public officers; plaintiff cannot sue for false light invasion of privacy if he or she is a public official and the publication relates to the performance of his or her public life or duties.

15. Torts ⚷8.5(5)

If publication presents public official's private life in a false light, he or she can sue under the false light tort, although actual malice must be shown.

16. Torts ⚷8.5(7)

Sheriff and deputies could not maintain false light invasion of privacy action against newspaper based on publication of matters relating to performance of official duties.

Witwer, Burlage, Poltrock & Giampietro by Wayne B. Giampietro, Chicago, Ill., and Marton & Hall, P.A. by Kraig J. Marton, Phoenix, for plaintiffs/appellants.

Gust, Rosenfeld & Henderson by James F. Henderson, Terrance C. Mead, Phoenix, for defendants/appellees.

Opinion of the Court of Appeals, Division One, 155 Ariz. 389, 746 P.2d 1319 (Ct.App. 1987) vacated.

FELDMAN, Vice Chief Justice.

Richard G. Godbehere, a former Maricopa County Sheriff, and several deputies and civilian employees of the sheriff's office (plaintiffs) brought this action against Phoenix Newspapers, Inc., the publisher of *The Arizona Republic* and *Phoenix Gazette*, and fourteen editors and reporters of the two newspapers (publishers), for libel and false light invasion of privacy. The trial court granted publishers' motion to dismiss for failure to state a claim as to the invasion of privacy claims, but refused to dismiss the other counts of the complaint. Plaintiffs appealed and the court of appeals affirmed. We granted review to determine whether Arizona should recognize a cause of action for false light invasion of privacy, and if so, what the proper standard should be. *See* Rule 23, Ariz.R.Civ.App.P., 17B A.R.S. We have jurisdiction pursuant to Ariz. Const. art. 6, § 5(3) and A.R.S. § 12–120.24.

FACTS

In the spring and summer of 1985, publishers printed over fifty articles, editorials, and columns (the publications) about plaintiffs' various law enforcement activities. The publications stated that the plaintiffs engaged in illegal activities, staged narcotics arrests to generate publicity, illegally arrested citizens, misused public funds and resources, committed police brutality, and generally were incompetent at law enforcement. Plaintiffs alleged in their eighteen-count complaint that the publications were false, damaged their reputations, harmed them in their profession, and caused them emotional distress.

Publishers moved to dismiss all eighteen counts of the complaint for failure to state a claim, and the court dismissed the false light invasion of privacy claims. In so doing, the trial court relied on *Rutledge v. Phoenix Newspapers, Inc.*, 148 Ariz. 555, 715 P.2d 1243 (Ct.App.1986), which held that a plaintiff must prove the elements of intentional infliction of emotional distress to claim false light invasion of privacy. The trial court found the acts in question were not so extreme or outrageous as to constitute the tort of intentional infliction of emotional distress. Minute Entry (filed June 18, 1986).

On appeal, plaintiffs argued that Arizona should follow the Restatement (Second) of Torts § 652E (1977) (hereafter Restatement), which provides in part:

> One who gives publicity to a matter concerning another that places the other before the public in a false light is subject to liability to the other for invasion of his privacy, if
>
> (a) the false light in which the other was placed would be highly offensive to a reasonable person, and
>
> (b) the actor had knowledge of or acted in reckless disregard as to the falsity of the publicized matter and the false light in which the other would be placed.

The court of appeals rejected the Restatement position as inconsistent with its own prior authority. *Godbehere v. Phoenix Newspapers, Inc.*, 155 Ariz. 389, 391, 746 P.2d 1319, 1321 (Ct.App.1987) (citing *Rutledge; Duhammel v. Star*, 133 Ariz. 558, 653 P.2d 15 (Ct.App.1982); *Cluff v. Farmers Insurance Exchange*, 10 Ariz.App. 560, 460 P.2d 666 (1969)).

We accepted plaintiffs' petition for review to decide whether Arizona should follow Restatement § 652E, recognizing the tort of false light invasion of privacy without requiring plaintiffs to prove all the elements of the tort of intentional infliction of emotional distress.

DISCUSSION

A. Development of the Right of Privacy

In 1890, Samuel Warren and Louis Brandeis published an article advocating the recognition of a right to privacy as an independent legal concept. Warren & Brandeis, *The Right to Privacy*, 4 HARV. L.REV. 193 (1890). Explaining how courts traditionally recognized claims involving injury to a person's private thoughts or feelings, they also described how courts used contract and property law to protect thoughts, ideas, or expressions from wrongful appropriation. *Id.* Warren and Brandeis contended these were nothing more than "instances and applications of a general right to privacy." *Id.* at 198. Hence, they supported recognition of the right "to be let alone." *Id.* at 203.

In 1905 the Georgia Supreme Court recognized the privacy right in a case involving wrongful appropriation of the plaintiff's name and likeness. *Pavesich v. New England Life Insurance Co.*, 50 S.E. 68 (Ga.1905). Controversy over recognition of a right to privacy continued, although the Restatement of Torts recognized an independent cause of action for interference with privacy in 1939. Restatement (First) of Torts § 867 (1939). A majority of jurisdictions eventually recognized the right in some form. PROSSER AND KEETON ON THE LAW OF TORTS § 117, at 850–51 (5th ed. 1984) (hereafter PROSSER & KEETON).

In 1960, Dean Prosser concluded that four separate torts had developed under the right of privacy rubric: (1) intrusion on the plaintiff's seclusion or private affairs; (2) public disclosure of embarrassing private facts; (3) publicity placing the plaintiff in a false light in the public eye; and (4) appropriation of the plaintiff's name or likeness for the defendant's advantage. Prosser, *Privacy,* 48 CALIF.L.REV. 383 (1960). In 1977, the Restatement adopted Prosser's classification. *See* Restatement § 652A–I (1977). Although each tort is classified under invasion of privacy, they "otherwise have almost nothing in common except that each represents an interference with the right of the plaintiff 'to be let alone.'" PROSSER & KEETON § 117, at 851.

B. Privacy in Arizona

Arizona first recognized an action for invasion of privacy in *Reed v. Real Detective Publishing Co.*, 63 Ariz. 294, 162 P.2d 133 (1945). *Reed* involved the unauthorized publication of the plaintiff's photograph. Subsequently, our court of appeals recognized the Restatement's four-part classification of the tort. *See Rutledge,* 148 Ariz. at 556, 715 P.2d at 1244; *Cluff,* 10 Ariz.App. at 563, 460 P.2d at 669.

Although most jurisdictions that recognize a cause of action for invasion of privacy have adopted the Restatement standard of "highly offensive to a reasonable person" or a similar standard, *see* Note, *Is Invasion of Privacy a Viable Cause of Action in Arizona?: Rethinking the Standard,* 30 ARIZ.L.REV. 319, 331 n. 96 (1988), Arizona courts of appeals' decisions have imposed a stricter standard. Rather than following the Restatement, these decisions have held that where the damage alleged is emotional, the plaintiff must prove the elements of the tort of intentional infliction of emotional distress in addition to proving invasion of privacy. To recover for invasion of privacy, a plaintiff must show that the defendant's conduct was "extreme and outrageous." [1] No other state requires a plaintiff to prove that the defendant committed "outrage" in a false light action. *See* Annotation, *False Light Invasion of Privacy–Cognizability and Elements,* 57 A.L.R.4th 22 (1987); Note, *supra,* 30 ARIZ.L.REV. at 338.

Publishers urge this court to adopt the court of appeals' view. They argue that there is no need for an independent tort of false light invasion of privacy because the action overlaps two other recognized torts: defamation and intentional infliction of emotional distress. These, publishers contend, cover the field and permit recovery in meritorious cases, thus making the false light action an unnecessary burden on the media's first amendment rights. To consider this argument, we must examine the distinctions between the false light action and the torts of intentional infliction of emotional distress and defamation.

C. False Light Invasion of Privacy and Intentional Infliction of Emotional Distress

Arizona has turned to Restatement § 46 to define intentional infliction of emotional distress, also known as the tort of outrage. *Ford v. Revlon, Inc.,* 153 Ariz. 38, 43, 734 P.2d 580, 585 (1987). This section provides:

> (1) one who by extreme and outrageous conduct intentionally or recklessly causes severe emotional distress to another is subject to liability for such emotional distress, and if bodily harm to the other results from it, for such bodily harm.

The element of "extreme and outrageous conduct" requires that plaintiff prove defendant's conduct exceeded "all bounds usually tolerated by decent society ... and [caused] mental distress of a very serious kind." PROSSER & KEETON § 12, at 60. This standard distinguishes "true claims from false ones, and ... the trifling insult or annoyance from the serious wrong." Prosser, *Mental Suffering,* 37 MICH.L. REV. 874, 877 (1939); *see also* Restatement § 46 comments b, d, and f.

The court of appeals has advanced two main reasons to justify imposing the intentional infliction standard on privacy actions. First, because the basis of the wrong in both outrage and invasion of privacy is infliction of mental suffering, the two torts are substantively similar and the same standard should apply to both. *Cluff,* 10 Ariz.App. at 564, 460 P.2d at 670; *see also Davis v. First National Bank of Arizona,* 124 Ariz. 458, 462–63, 605 P.2d 37, 41–42 (Ct.App.1979). Second, the court suggested that the rule was necessary to prevent plaintiffs from circumventing the "stringent standards necessary to otherwise establish a claim for the intentional infliction of emotional distress." *Rutledge,* 148 Ariz. at 557, 715 P.2d at 1245. This stricter standard was necessary "to protect defendants from unwarranted lawsuits." *Duhammel,* 133 Ariz. at 561, 653 P.2d at 18.

1. Arizona cases applying the intentional infliction "extreme and outrageous conduct" standard to invasion of privacy claims include: *Godbehere v. Phoenix Newspapers,* 155 Ariz. 389, 746 P.2d 1319 (Ct.App.1987) (false light); *Hirsch v. Cooper,* 153 Ariz. 454, 737 P.2d 1092 (Ct.App. 1986) (false light); *Rutledge v. Phoenix Newspapers, Inc.,* 148 Ariz. 555, 715 P.2d 1243 (Ct.App. 1986) (private facts, false light); *Creamer v. Raffety,* 145 Ariz. 34, 699 P.2d 908 (Ct.App.1985) (intrusion); *Valencia v. Duval Corp.,* 132 Ariz. 348, 645 P.2d 1262 (Ct.App.1982) (intrusion); *Duhammel v. Star,* 133 Ariz. 558, 653 P.2d 15 (Ct.App.1982) (false light); *Davis v. First National Bank of Arizona,* 124 Ariz. 458, 605 P.2d 37 (Ct.App.1979) (intrusion); *Cluff v. Farmer's Insurance Exchange,* 10 Ariz.App. 560, 460 P.2d 666 (1969) (intrusion).

Here, as in the above cases, the trial court dismissed plaintiffs' privacy claims for failure to state a cause of action, relying on *Rutledge* and holding that the acts of which plaintiffs complained were not outrageous. Minute Entry (filed June 18, 1986). Assuming the court was correct on the evidence, we must determine whether it correctly required plaintiffs to prove the tort of outrage in a privacy action.

[1] Publishers emphasize that actions for both intentional infliction of emotional distress and invasion of privacy provide compensation for emotional distress or damage to sensibility. *Cf.* Restatement §§ 46 and 652E. Thus, the injury from both torts is similar. Although this may be true, the fact that two different actions address the same injury is no reason to refuse to recognize torts that protect against different wrongful conduct. For example, three victims may suffer broken legs in the following ways: (1) a defendant negligently drives a car into the first victim's car; (2) a defendant's defective product injures the second victim; and (3) a defendant, without justification, attacks the third. Each victim would have a different tort claim: negligence, strict liability, and battery. The fact that each victim suffers the same type of injury does not preclude recognizing separate tort actions. Each tort theory developed separately to deter and provide redress against a different type of wrongful conduct.

[2] Thus, the fact that outrage and invasion of privacy both provide redress for emotional injury does not persuade us that the actions are "merged" or that plaintiffs should be required to prove the former in an action for the latter. The outrage tort protects against conduct so extreme that it would induce "an average member of the community ... to exclaim, 'outrageous!' " Restatement § 46 comment d. False light invasion of privacy, however, protects against the conduct of knowingly *or recklessly* publishing false information or innuendo that a "reasonable person" would find "highly offensive." Although false publication may constitute outrageous conduct and vice versa, it is also true that the same wrongful conduct will not always satisfy the elements of both tort actions. *See* Note, *supra*, 30 ARIZ.L.REV. at 342. Because each action protects against a different type of tortious conduct, each has its place, and the common injury should not abrogate the action. *See id.*

[3] Nor do we believe that recognizing the false light action without requiring plaintiffs to prove outrage will circumvent the "stringent standards" of the emotional distress tort. *See Rutledge*, 148 Ariz. at 557, 715 P.2d at 1245. The standards for proving false light invasion of privacy are quite "stringent" by themselves. For example, the plaintiff in a false light case must prove that the defendant published with knowledge of the falsity or reckless disregard for the truth. *See* Restatement § 652E. This standard is as stringent as the intentional infliction of emotional distress requirement that the plaintiff prove the defendant "intentionally or recklessly caused" the emotional distress. *See* Restatement § 46.

[4] We also do not share the court of appeals' concern with creating unwarranted lawsuits. Freeing a plaintiff from the need to prove outrageous conduct in a privacy suit does not require us to provide a remedy for "every trivial indignity." *See* Prosser, *supra*, 37 MICH.L.REV. at 877. A defendant is not liable in a false light case unless the publication places the plaintiff in a false light highly offensive to a reasonable person. *Time, Inc. v. Hill*, 385 U.S. 374, 87 S.Ct. 534, 17 L.Ed.2d 456 (1967); Restatement § 652E. Thus, the plaintiff's subjective threshold of sensibility is not the measure, and "trivial indignities" are not actionable.

[5] We conclude, therefore, that the two torts exist to redress different types of wrongful conduct. Situations exist where a jury could find the defendant's publication of false information or innuendo was not outrageous but did satisfy the false light elements. *See* Zimmerman, *False Light Invasion of Privacy: The Light That Failed*, 64 N.Y.U.L.REV. 364 (1989). Thus, we believe the tort action for false

light invasion of privacy provides protection against a narrow class of wrongful conduct that falls short of "outrage," but nevertheless should be deterred.

D. Invasion of Privacy and Defamation

A second argument advanced by publishers is that little distinction exists between a tort action for false light invasion of privacy and one for defamation. Thus, because defamation actions are available, they argue, Arizona need not recognize false light invasion of privacy. Again, we disagree.

[6–9] Although both defamation and false light invasion of privacy involve publication, the nature of the interests protected by each action differs substantially. *See* PROSSER & KEETON § 117, at 864. A defamation action compensates *damage to reputation* or good name caused by the publication of false information. *Hill*, 385 U.S. at 384 n. 9, 87 S.Ct. at 540 n. 9; *Reed*. To be defamatory, a publication must be false and must bring the defamed person into disrepute, contempt, or ridicule, or must impeach plaintiff's honesty, integrity, virtue, or reputation. *See Phoenix Newspapers, Inc. v. Choisser*, 82 Ariz. 271, 312 P.2d 150 (1957).

Privacy, on the other hand, does not protect reputation but protects mental and emotional interests. Indeed, "[t]he gravamen of [a privacy] action ... is the injury to the feelings of the plaintiff, the mental anguish and distress caused by the publication." *Reed*, 63 Ariz. at 305, 162 P.2d at 139. The remedy is available "to protect a person's interest in being let alone and is available when there has been publicity of a kind that is highly offensive." PROSSER & KEETON § 117, at 864. Under this theory, a plaintiff may recover even in the absence of reputational damage, as long as the publicity is unreasonably offensive and attributes false characteristics. However, to qualify as a false light invasion of privacy, the publication must involve "a major misrepresentation of [the plaintiff's] character, history, activities or beliefs," not merely minor or unimportant inaccuracies. Restatement § 652E comment c.

[10, 11] Another distinction between defamation and false light invasion of privacy is the role played by truth. To be defamatory, a publication must be false, and truth is a defense. PROSSER & KEETON § 116, at 839. A false light cause of action may arise when something untrue has been published about an individual, *see* PROSSER & KEETON § 117, at 863–66, *or* when the publication of true information creates a false implication about the individual. In the latter type of case, the false innuendo created by the highly offensive presentation of a true fact constitutes the injury.[2] *See* Restatement § 652E.

Thus, although defamation and false light often overlap, they serve very different objectives. The two tort actions deter different conduct and redress different wrongs. A plaintiff may bring a false light invasion of privacy action even though the publication is not defamatory, and even though the actual facts stated are true. Several examples in comment b to Restatement § 652E also illustrate the practical differences between a false light action and defamation and demonstrate how, in a cer-

2. A good example of a false light cause of action based on implication is *Douglass v. Hustler Magazine, Inc.*, 769 F.2d 1128 (7th Cir.1985), *cert. denied*, 475 U.S. 1094, 106 S.Ct. 1489, 89 L.Ed.2d 892 (1986). In *Douglass*, the plaintiff posed nude, consenting to the publication of her photographs in *Playboy* magazine. Her photographer subsequently left the employ of *Playboy* for *Hustler* magazine, a publication of much lower standing in the journalistic community. He sold her photographs to *Hustler*, which published them. The plaintiff sued for the nonconsensual use of the photographs. Plaintiff had no cause of action for defamation, because essentially, there was nothing untrue about the photographs. She posed for them and, as published, they did not misrepresent her. She also had no claim for outrage. She voluntarily posed for the photographs and consented to their publication in *Playboy*. Publication was not "outrageous," as it may have been if she were photographed without her knowledge and the photos published without her initial consent. However, the court upheld her recovery for false light invasion of privacy. The jury may have focused on the differences between *Playboy* and *Hustler* and concluded that to be published in *Hustler*, as if she had posed for that publication, falsely placed her in a different light than the *Playboy* publication. 769 F.2d at 1138.

tain class of cases, the false light action is the only redress available.[3] It is these considerations, we believe, that lead the vast majority of other jurisdictions, including the United States Supreme Court, to recognize the distinction between defamation and false light.[4]

E. Arizona and the False Light Tort

[12] Momentarily leaving aside the free speech considerations, we are persuaded to recognize the distinct tort of false light invasion of privacy as articulated by Restatement § 652E.[5] The argument that recognition of this action invites much new litigation is of questionable merit. To date, only four cases of false light privacy have been presented in Arizona, including the instant case. States recognizing the false light action have not been deluged with substantially more litigation than afflicts this state. In most cases, the false light theory will add little if anything beyond the relief a defamation or emotional distress claim will provide. Some cases exist, however, where the theory will protect a small area otherwise lacking protection against invasion of privacy. That interest, we believe, demands protection.

Arizona is one of the first states whose founders thought it necessary to adopt explicit protection for the privacy of its citizens. *See* Ariz. Const. art. 2, § 8. Unless the interest in protecting privacy rights is outweighed by the interest in protecting speech, *see Mountain States Telephone & Telegraph Co. v. Arizona Corporation Commission*, 160 Ariz. 350, 773 P.2d 455 (1989), we see no reason not to recognize an action for false light invasion of privacy.

F. Free Speech Considerations

[13] As in defamation, a public official in a false light action must always show that the defendant published with knowledge of the false innuendo or with reckless disregard of the truth. *See* Restatement § 652E comment b. Any doubt about the application of the actual malice element of the false light tort to public figures has been eliminated. In *Hustler Magazine, Inc. v. Falwell*, 485 U.S. 46, 108 S.Ct. 876, 99 L.Ed.2d 41 (1988), the Supreme Court held that a public figure plaintiff must prove *Times v. Sullivan* actual malice in order to recover for intentional infliction of emotional distress. Although *Hustler* was an intentional infliction case, the language used by the Court is so broad that it applies

3. Restatement § 652E comment b gives the following illustrations:

> 3. A is a renowned poet. B publishes in his magazine a spurious inferior poem, signed with A's name. Regardless of whether the poem is so bad as to subject B to liability for libel, B is subject to liability to A for invasion of privacy. [This example is presumably based on the case from which the false light concept arose—*Lord Byron v. Johnston*, 2 Mer. 29, 35 Eng.Rep. 851 (1816).]
>
> 4. A is a Democrat. B induces him to sign a petition nominating C for office. A discovers that C is a Republican and demands that B remove his name from the petition. B refuses to do so and continues public circulation of the petition, bearing A's name. B is subject to liability to A for invasion of privacy.
>
> 5. A is a war hero, distinguished for bravery in a famous battle. B makes and exhibits a motion picture concerning A's life, in which he inserts a detailed narrative of a fictitious private life attributed to A, including a non-existent romance with a girl. B knows this matter to be false. Although A is not defamed by the motion picture, B is subject to liability to him for invasion of privacy.

Illustrations 3, 4, and 5.

4. *Hill*, 385 U.S. at 384 n. 9, 87 S.Ct. at 540 n. 9; *Wood v. Hustler Magazine, Inc.*, 736 F.2d 1084 (5th Cir.1984), *cert. denied*, 469 U.S. 1107, 105 S.Ct. 783, 83 L.Ed.2d 777 (1985); *Rinsley v. Brandt*, 700 F.2d 1304 (10th Cir.1983); *Dodrill v. Arkansas Democrat Co.*, 265 Ark. 628, 590 S.W.2d 840 (1979), *cert. denied*, 444 U.S. 1076, 100 S.Ct. 1024, 62 L.Ed.2d 759 (1980); *Selleck v. Globe International, Inc.*, 166 Cal.App.3d 1123, 212 Cal.Rptr. 838 (1985); *Goodrich v. Waterbury Republican-American, Inc.*, 188 Conn. 107, 448 A.2d 1317 (1982); *Anderson v. Low Rent Housing Commission*, 304 N.W.2d 239 (Iowa 1981); *Froelich v. Adair*, 213 Kan. 357, 516 P.2d 993 (1973); *McCall v. Courier-Journal and Louisville Times Co.*, 623 S.W.2d 882 (Ky.1981), *cert. denied*, 456 U.S. 975, 102 S.Ct. 2239, 72 L.Ed.2d 849 (1982); *McCormack v. Oklahoma Publishing Co.*, 613 P.2d 737 (Okl.1980); *see also* Annot., *supra*, 57 A.L.R.4th 22, §§ 7–12.

5. Insofar as there is contrary language in *Rutledge, Duhammel*, and other Arizona false light cases, we disapprove the decisions.

to any tort action relating to free speech, particularly "in the area of public debate about public figures." *See Hustler*, 485 U.S. at 53, 108 S.Ct. at 881.[6] Additional protection for free speech comes from the principle that protection for privacy interests generally applies only to private matters. *See* Restatement § 652A comment b; *Reed*, 63 Ariz. at 304, 162 P.2d at 138.

G. Is False Light Available in This Case?

Finally, publishers contended that even if we recognize false light actions, the action does not lie in this case. They argue that not only do the publications discuss matters of public interest, but plaintiffs have no right of privacy with respect to the manner in which they perform their official duties. We agree.

[14, 15] We have specifically held that the right of privacy does not exist "where the plaintiff has become a public character...." *Reed*, 63 Ariz. at 304, 162 P.2d at 138. In addition, privacy rights are absent or limited "in connection with the life of a person in whom the public has a rightful interest, [or] where the information would be of public benefit." *Reed*, 63 Ariz. at 304, 162 P.2d at 138; *see also Cox Broadcasting Corp. v. Cohn*, 420 U.S. 469, 490, 95 S.Ct. 1029, 1044, 43 L.Ed.2d 328 (1975) (relying on *Hill*, 385 U.S. at 388, 87 S.Ct. at 542); *Reardon v. News–Journal Co.*, 53 Del. 29, 164 A.2d 263, 267 (1960); *Meyer v. Ledford*, 170 Ga.App. 245, 316 S.E.2d 804 (1984); *Adreani v. Hansen*, 80 Ill.App.3d 726, 36 Ill.Dec. 259, 400 N.E.2d 679 (1980).

A number of jurisdictions take the position that because false light is a form of invasion of privacy, it must relate only to the private affairs of the plaintiff and cannot involve matters of public interest. *See* Annot., *supra*, 57 A.L.R.4th 22, § 10. It is difficult to conceive of an area of greater public interest than law enforcement. Certainly the public has a legitimate interest in the manner in which law enforcement officers perform their duties. Therefore, we hold that there can be no false light invasion of privacy action for matters involving official acts or duties of public officers.

Consequently, we adopt the following legal standard: a plaintiff cannot sue for false light invasion of privacy if he or she is a public official *and* the publication relates to performance of his or her public life or duties. We do not go so far as to say, however, that a public official has no privacy rights at all and may never bring an action for invasion of privacy. Certainly, if the publication presents the public official's private life in a false light, he or she can sue under the false light tort, although actual malice must be shown.

[16] The Supreme Court has held that "the public official designation applies at the very least to those among the hierarchy of government employees who have, or appear to the public to have, substantial responsibility for or control over the conduct of governmental affairs." *Rosenblatt v. Baer*, 383 U.S. 75, 85, 86 S.Ct. 669, 676, 15 L.Ed.2d 597 (1966). Police and other law enforcement personnel are almost always classified as public officials. *See, e.g., Time, Inc. v. Pape*, 401 U.S. 279, 291–92, 91 S.Ct. 633, 640–41, 28 L.Ed.2d 45 (1971) (deputy chief of detectives); *St. Amant v. Thompson*, 390 U.S. 727, 730, 88 S.Ct. 1323, 1325, 20 L.Ed.2d 262 (1968) (deputy sheriff); *Henry v. Collins*, 380 U.S. 356, 357, 85 S.Ct. 992, 993, 13 L.Ed.2d 892 (1965) (per curiam) (city police chief and county attorney); *Gray v. Udevitz*, 656 F.2d 588 (10th Cir.1981) (ex-patrolman); *Meiners v. Moriarity*, 563 F.2d 343, 352 (7th Cir.1977) (federal DEA agent); *Rosales v. City of Eloy*, 122 Ariz. 134, 135, 593 P.2d 688, 689 (1979) (police sergeant); *Roche v. Egan*, 433 A.2d 757, 762 (Me.1981) (all law en-

6. To this point, we have spoken of false light as requiring that the plaintiff show actual malice. Restatement § 652E seems to state that requirement, but the Caveat to section 652E states that the Institute "takes no position" on whether, under some circumstances, a non-public figure may recover for false light invasion of privacy where he does not show actual malice but does show negligent publication. *See also* Restatement § 652E comment on Clause (b). Because this case does not present the issue, we also take no position on the validity of a false light action for negligent publication. Suffice it to say that in this case, where we deal with publications concerning public officers performing public duties, the first amendment controls.

forcement personnel). The sheriff and the deputies here are public officials.[7] The publications at issue concern the discharge of their public duties and do not relate to private affairs. Therefore, plaintiffs have no claim for false light invasion of privacy.

We affirm the trial court's dismissal of the false light claim. Because we disagree with the court of appeals' reasoning, we vacate that opinion and remand to the trial court for further proceedings consistent with this opinion.

GORDON, C.J., and CAMERON and MOELLER, JJ., concur.

HOLOHAN, J., retired before the decision of this case.

CORCORAN, J., did not participate in the determination of this case.

Cite as
96 Ariz. Adv. Rep. 43

IN THE COURT OF APPEALS
STATE OF ARIZONA
DIVISION ONE

Melissa D. VAN CAMP, a minor child, by and through her next friend and parents, Greg Van Camp and Tammy Van Camp; Greg Van Camp and Tammy Van Camp, husband and wife,
Plaintiffs-Appellants,
v.
ICG MANAGEMENT COMPANY, a California corporation; Intercontinental Company, a California corporation; Bel Air Savings and Loan, a California partnership,
Defendants-Appellees.

No. 1 CA-CV 89-456
DEPARTMENT A
FILED: September 24, 1991

Appeal from the Superior Court of Maricopa County, Cause No. CV 87-40805, The Honorable Susan R. Bolton, Judge

REVERSED AND REMANDED

ATTORNEYS:

Charles, Keist & Thompson, P.C., by Joseph W. Charles, Attorneys for Plaintiffs-Appellants, Glendale

Stinson & Roberts, P.A., by Edwin R. Roberts, Attorneys for Defendants-Appellees, Phoenix

CONTRERAS, Judge

This is an appeal from the trial court's order granting summary judgment in favor of the owners and managers of an apartment complex (hereinafter referred to collectively as appellees), in a personal injury action stemming from injuries that three-year old Melissa Van Camp sustained when she fell from a bedroom window in her parents' apartment. Because we conclude there are factual issues to be resolved, we reverse the trial court's order granting summary judgment and remand for further proceedings.

FACTS AND PROCEDURAL HISTORY

On review from the trial court's order granting summary judgment, the facts are viewed in the light most favorable to the party against whom the judgment was entered. *Wagenseller v. Scottsdale Memorial Hosp.*, 147 Ariz. 370,

388, 710 P.2d 1025, 1043 (1985). The appellants are Greg and Tammy Van Camp and their daughter Melissa. Melissa was injured when she fell from the bedroom window of her parents' apartment, a distance of approximately twenty feet and seven inches.[1] At the time of her fall, Melissa was approximately three years and ten months of age.

Melissa's parents inspected the apartment before renting it and had lived there for approximately six months prior to Melissa's fall. The bedroom window from which Melissa fell was located, at its lowest point, twenty-four inches from the floor. There was an exterior window screen covering the bedroom window.

On the day of Melissa's fall, Tammy Van Kamp was taking care of her niece Megan. Tammy went into the bedroom where Megan was in a crib. She opened the bedroom window and began to change Megan's diaper. Melissa was also in the bedroom with Tammy talking to Megan. Tammy then telephoned her mother and began talking with her. Melissa continued to talk and play with Megan and was moving back and forth between the crib and the open bedroom window. As Tammy continued her conversation, she heard the window screen give way and saw Melissa fall out the bedroom window.

Appellants filed suit against appellees, the general contractor who constructed the apartment, and the architect who designed the apartment alleging various causes of action, including negligence.[2] Appellees moved for summary judgment on the negligence claim and the trial court granted this motion by order. The trial court, citing *McFarland v. Kahn*, 123 Ariz. 62, 597 P.2d 544 (1979), ruled that the duty owed by appellees is the duty to take those reasonable precautions for the safety of the tenant as would be taken by reasonably prudent persons under similar circumstances. The trial court found that the window was open and obvious and not unreasonably dangerous and therefore appellees could not be held liable due to the location of the window. The trial court further found that the appellees had no notice that the window screen would not hold the weight of a three-year old child and therefore had no duty to warn or repair. Appellants timely appealed the trial court's order granting appellees' motion for summary judgment.

DISCUSSION

The question presented is whether the trial court was correct in granting the appellees' motion for summary judgment on appellants' negligence claim. It is unclear whether the trial court ruled that because the window was open and obvious and not unreasonably dangerous, appellees had no duty or, whether the trial court ruled that although appellees had a duty, appellees did not, as a matter of law, breach that duty. Accordingly, we must review the standard for granting a motion for summary judgment in a negligence action as well as the duty owed by a landlord to tenants' children.

On appeal, appellants argue that the trial court erred in granting appellees' motion for summary judgment because questions of fact exist. Appellants argue that appellees were negligent in renting to a family with young children a third floor apartment with a window located twenty-four inches from the floor, without the proper safeguards to prevent young children from falling out. Appellants argue that the location of the window and the ease in which the window screen gave way under Melissa's weight constituted hidden perils. These conditions, appellants assert, created a foreseeable and unreasonable risk to a child of Melissa's age. Appellants assert that the testimony of two expert witnesses[3] affirmatively demonstrates the defective design of the window and therefore creates questions of fact that should be reserved for trial. Appellants further argue that the mere fact that a condition is open and obvious does not preclude it from being unreasonably dangerous.

With respect to the window screen, appellants offered expert testimony on the alleged improper screening of the window from which Melissa fell. Appellants also offered expert testimony on whether appellees had knowledge of this condition from the number of other window screens appellants alleged were lying around the apartment complex. Lastly, appellants argue that the trial court improperly imputed to Melissa her parents' knowledge of the window as an open and obvious danger. Appellants contend that Melissa was too young to be found contributorily negligent and that her parents' alleged negligence cannot be imputed to Melissa.

Appellees argue in response, that if a condition is open and obvious to the tenant, it is not, as a matter of law, unreasonably dangerous. Appellees contend the window was not a condition likely to cause harm since it complied with all building codes and the condition was an open and obvious condition to Melissa's parents. Moreover, appellees argue that appellants created a dangerous condition when Melissa's mother opened the window and allowed Melissa to play in close proximity to it. Lastly, appellees argue that there was no evidence that appellees had notice that the window screen would not hold a three-year old child and therefore, appellees cannot be liable.

MOTION FOR SUMMARY JUDGMENT

The granting of a motion for summary judgment is proper "when the evidence presents no genuine issue of material fact." *Orme School v. College World Services, Inc.*, 166 Ariz. 301, 305, 802 P.2d 1000, 1004 (1990). The *Orme* court noted that it is in the common law tort claim that "the jury is given the most deference in weighing evidence, drawing inferences, and reaching conclusions on questions of negligence, causation and damages." *Id.* at 310, 802 P.2d at 1009. A plaintiff in a tort action need prove his claim only by a preponderance of the evidence. *Id.* Summary judgment is inappropriate where the trial court would be required to pass on the credibility of witnesses with different versions of the material facts, would be required to weigh the quality of documentary or other evidence, and would be required to choose between competing or conflicting inferences. *Id.* at 311, 802 P.2d at 1010. However, the trial court may properly grant a motion for summary judgment where the evidence is such that no reasonable jury could conclude, by a preponderance of the evidence, that the defendant was actively responsible for plaintiff's injury. *Id.* at 311, 802 P.2d at 1010. In the case before us, we must determine whether the evidence put forth by the appellants was such that no reasonable jury could find that appellees were actively responsible for Melissa's injury.

NEGLIGENCE

In order to maintain a negligence claim, a plaintiff must show (1) a duty recognized by law, which requires the defendant to conform to a certain standard of conduct, (2) a breach of that duty, (3) a causal connection between the breach of that duty and the injury, and (4) actual injury or damage. *Ontiveros v. Borak*, 136 Ariz. 500, 504, 667 P.2d 200, 204 (1983)(citing W. Prosser, *Handbook on the Law of Torts*, §30, at 143 (4th ed. 1971)). The question of duty is a question of law for the court. *Markowitz v. Arizona Parks Bd.*, 146 Ariz. 352, 706 P.2d 364 (1985). The determining factor is whether the relationship of the parties is such that the defendant was under an obligation to use some care to avoid or prevent injury to the plaintiff. *Markowitz*, 146 Ariz. at 356, 706 P.2d at 368. If such a relationship does not exist, the defendant is not under any duty and therefore is not liable. *Id.*

Appellees argue that a landlord has the duty to protect a child from hazards on the property "... only if (1) he knows of a condition which is probably going to harm the child and (2) the tenant, although they may have knowledge of the condition, cannot prevent the harm from occurring." Appellees further argue that if a condition is open and obvious, that as a matter of law, a landlord owes no duty to a tenant. Appellees cite *Presson v. Mountain States Properties, Inc.*, 18 Ariz. App. 176, 501 P.2d 17 (1972); *McLeod v. Newcomer*, 163 Ariz. 6, 785 P.2d 575 (App. 1989); and *Udy v. Calvary Corp.*, 162 Ariz. 7, 780 P.2d 1055 (App. 1989) in support of this proposition. We disagree.

The initial question is whether the relationship between the appellees and Melissa was such that appellees were under an obligation to use some care to avoid or prevent injury to Melissa. *Markowitz*, 146 Ariz. at 356, 706 P.2d at 368. Although the lease agreement between the parties is not contained in the record, it can be inferred from the record that Melissa resided with her parents in the apartment with the knowledge and consent of the appellees and therefore is a tenant. In *McFarland* the plaintiff was a twelve-year old boy who was injured by a sprinkler in the common area of the apartment complex where he resided. The Arizona Supreme Court held that the case was controlled by *Cummings v. Prater*, 95 Ariz. 20, 27, 386 P.2d 27, 31 (1963), a case in which the court held that the duty of the landlord is to "take those precautions for the safety of the tenant as would be taken by a reasonably prudent man under similar circumstances." The *McFarland* case does not distinguish the duties owed by a landlord to an adult residing on the premises versus a child residing on the premises. Accordingly, appellees owed the same duty to Melissa as they would to any other tenant. Appellees' duty does not arise from the combination of appellees' knowledge of the condition and the parents' inability to protect Melissa from the condition, but rather arises from the appellees' landlord-tenant relationship with Melissa. *See also McLeod*, 163 Ariz. 6, 785 P.2d 575 (two-year old child residing in home of parents injured after falling in swimming pool a tenant); *Udy*, 162 Ariz. 7, 780 P.2d 1055 (landlord's duty to seven-year old child living with his parents is not circumscribed by physical boundaries of the landlord's property).

Furthermore, the question of whether a condition is open and obvious is not relevant to the question of the existence of a duty. As previously noted, appellees' duty to Melissa arises from the landlord-tenant relationship. *McLeod*, 163 Ariz. at 9, 785 P.2d at 578. The Arizona Supreme Court stated in *Markowitz*, 146 Ariz. at 356, 706 P.2d at 368:

> [T]he possibility that the defect or hazard is 'open and obvious' is a factor to be considered in determining whether the possessor's failure to remedy the hazard or provide a warning was unreasonable and therefore breached the standard of care; it is not a factor to be used in determining the very existence of the duty which is a precondition for the exercise of the standard of care.... [W]here the possessor should foresee that the condition is dangerous despite its open and obvious nature, neither the obvious nature nor the plaintiff's knowledge

of the danger is conclusive. (citations omitted).

We recognize that *Markowitz* involved a possessor-invitee relationship. However, we believe that the court's analysis on the irrelevance of the open and obvious nature of a condition to the initial determination of the existence of a duty is equally applicable to the landlord-tenant relationship. *See McLeod*, 163 Ariz. at 11, 785 P.2d at 580 ("landlord's duty to a tenant analogous to that of a property owner to an invitee")("the open and obvious nature of the dangerous aspects of a swimming pool would not necessarily relieve a landlord of liability to a child")(citing *Schultz v. Eslick*, 788 F.2d 558 (9th Cir. 1986)); *Cummings v. Prater*, 95 Ariz. 20, 27, 386 P.2d 27, 31 (whether a condition is open and obvious is merely a factor in considering whether a condition is unreasonably dangerous). We conclude that appellees owed Melissa a duty to use care to avoid or prevent injury to her.

STANDARD OF CARE

Once a duty on the part of the defendant has been established, the question becomes whether defendant's conduct met the required standard of care. The Arizona Supreme Court has characterized a landlord's duty to a tenant as the duty to take those precautions for the safety of the tenant as would be taken by a reasonably prudent person under similar circumstances. *Cummings*, 95 Ariz. at 26, 386 P.2d at 31. Accordingly, we hold that the duty owed by a landlord to a child tenant is the duty to exercise such care as a reasonably prudent person would exercise toward a child tenant under similar circumstances. *McFarland*, 123 Ariz. at 63, 597 P.2d at 545; *Udy*, 162 Ariz. at 11-12, 780 P.2d at 1059-60; *McLeod*, 163 Ariz. at 9, 785 P.2d at 578. Appellees therefore had the duty to exercise such care as a reasonably prudent person would when renting a third floor apartment to a family with small children, equipped with a screen of the type that was on appellants' window.

While the duty of the landlord to a child tenant is the same as the duty to an adult tenant, the *conduct* necessary to fulfill the landlord's duty may vary.

> The characteristics of children are proper matters for consideration in determining what is ordinary care with respect to them, and there may be a duty to take precautions with respect to those of tender years which would not be necessary in the care of adults. The duty is to exercise such care as a reasonably prudent person would exercise toward children under like circumstances.

Shannon v. Butler Homes, Inc., 102 Ariz. 312, 317, 428 P.2d 990, 995 (1967); *see also McLeod*, 163 Ariz. at 9, 785 P.2d at 578; *Udy*, 162 Ariz. at 14, 780 P.2d at 1062.

Appellees rely most heavily on the fact that the height of the window above the floor was open and obvious to Melissa's parents. Although it is generally accepted that a defendant is not liable for injuries resulting from a condition that is open and obvious and that is or should be known to the plaintiff, the open and obvious nature of a hazard is only one factor to be considered in determining whether a defendant is negligent. *See Udy*, 162 Ariz. at 14, 780 P.2d at 1062; *Cummings*, 95 Ariz. at 27, 386 P.2d at 31. Moreover, while there may be little doubt that the height of the window and any resulting danger was open and obvious to Melissa's parents, the more relevant inquiry in the present case is whether the condition was open and obvious to Melissa as a tenant. *McLeod*, 163 Ariz. at 11, 785 P.2d at 580.

The determination of whether a condition is open and obvious is generally a question of fact. *Tribe v. Shell Oil Co., Inc.*, 133 Ariz. 517, 519, 652 P.2d 1040, 1042 (1982); *Andrews v. Casagrande*, 167 Ariz. 71, 804 P.2d 800 (App. 1990); *McLeod*, 163 Ariz. at 10, 785 P.2d at 579 (whether the unfenced swimming pool constituted an open and obvious condition is a question that is inappropriate to resolve as a question of law); *Shaw v. Peterson*, 88 Ariz. Adv. Rep. 8 (Arizona Court of Appeals, June 11, 1991) (reasonable minds could differ on whether an unfenced swimming pool constituted a hidden peril to a nineteen-month old child). We conclude that whether the condition was open and obvious to Melissa is not a question of law but a question of fact. *McLeod*, 163 Ariz. at 9-10, 785 P.2d at 582-83. The fact that a child resides with parents does not transfer the landlord's obligation to the child to the child's parents. *Id.* at 10, 785 P.2d at 579. It is just an additional factor for the trier of fact to consider in determining whether the landlord breached the duty of care to the child. Moreover, the danger in the present case was the *combination* of the low window and what appears to be a screen which was not secure.

The appellees claim that it is unforeseeable that a third story window would result in harm, and that it had no reason to know that appellants would open the window and allow Melissa to play near it. A defendant is only liable for injuries resulting from foreseeable risks of harm. *Bach v. State*, 152 Ariz. 145, 148, 730 P.2d 854, 857 (App. 1986)("once a duty is established, the foreseeability of harm governs the scope of that duty."); *see also Udy*, 162 Ariz. at 14, 780 P.2d at 1062. Although in *some* cases "it may be said ... as a matter of law that defendant's actions or inactions do not breach the applicable standard of conduct," it is where reasonable minds could differ on the underlying question of whether the risk of injury is foreseeable that the question of negligence is one of fact. *Markowitz*, 146 Ariz. at 357, 706 P.2d at 369 (emphasis added); *Orme*, 166 Ariz. 301, 802 P.2d 1000. Although it may be unforeseeable that an adult would fall through a low, screened window, reasonable minds could differ on the foreseeability that a young child could be injured in that manner. Despite the appellees' claim that it had no reason to know that the window would be opened, where the window is the type that opens and has a screen which would be necessary only if it *was* opened, reasonable minds could conclude that it was foreseeable that the window would be opened. In addition, even though an adult might be expected to exercise caution in the presence of a low, open window, a young child might not appreciate the risk and therefore would not know to exercise the necessary caution. *See State v. Juengel*, 15 Ariz. App. 495, 497-98, 489 P.2d 869, 871-72 (App. 1971).

Appellees point out that there is no evidence in the record that it had any notice that the screen would not hold a child's weight. Therefore, the argument continues, they had no reason to suspect the dangerous condition. *See, e.g., Shirkey v. Crain & Assocs. Management Co., Inc.*, 129 Ariz. 128, 629 P.2d 95 (App. 1981)(defendant not liable where defect in bathtub grab-bar was not apparent by looking at it). Despite language in *Cummings* that a landlord's duty is "to inspect the premises *when he has reason to suspect defects* ...," 95 Ariz. at 26, 686 P.2d at 31 (emphasis added), subsequent cases have emphasized the language in *Cummings* stating that a landlord "is under a duty to take those precautions for the safety of the tenant as would be taken by a reasonably prudent man under similar circumstances." *Id.*; *see McFarland v. Kahn*, 123 Ariz. at 62, 597 P.2d at 544; *Udy*, 162 Ariz. at 11-12, 780 P.2d at 1059-60; *McLeod*, 163 Ariz. at 8, 785 P.2d at 577; *see also Presson v. Mountain States Prop., Inc.*, 18 Ariz. App. at 178, 501 P.2d at 19. Under this standard, reasonable minds could conclude that a reasonably prudent landlord faced with the circumstances of this case, a family with a small child, a third story apartment, and a low window, might take some type of precaution for the safety of the child tenants. *Possible* courses of action could include checking the safety of the screen, installing a protective grill, or taking other preventative measures.

Reasonable minds could also conclude that a screened window appears safer than an unscreened window, and that the presence of the screen created an illusion of safety. It is worth noting that appellees claim on the one hand that it had no notice that the screen could not retain a child's weight, and on the other, that anyone would know a screen is intended to keep insects out, rather than retain the weight of a child. Although an adult would probably recognize this, a young child might not. The reasonableness of appellees' conduct must be examined in the context of their duty to Melissa, as opposed to her parents.

Finally, appellants argue that the trial court based its ruling, in part, on the alleged contributory negligence of Melissa. A reading of the trial court's ruling, however, demonstrates that it was based on the belief that the appellees were not liable as a matter of law. The ruling does not refer to contributory negligence and does not appear to be based on any conclusions about either Melissa's alleged contributory negligence, or that of her parents. It is therefore not necessary to reach this issue.

Before concluding this decision, it is appropriate to discuss the dissenting opinion and direct a few comments to the dissent. In reading and considering the majority and dissenting opinions, one fundamental proposition must be kept in mind. This Court (majority) is merely reversing the trial court's grant of summary judgment to the appellees (landlords). The present opinion is predicated upon Arizona Supreme court decisions that summary judgment is inappropriate when the record demonstrates that the evidence presents genuine issues of material fact. *Orme*, 166 Ariz. 301, 802 P.2d 1000; *Markowitz*, 146 Ariz. 352, 706 P.2d 364. As extensively discussed in the preceding sections, such a record is presented here. This Court (majority) does not in any manner pass on the merits of this case. We simply hold that the appellees owed Melissa a duty and that the plaintiffs have put forth sufficient evidence to create factual questions to be resolved by the jury.

After considering all the evidence in the present case, a jury might conclude that the injury was not foreseeable or that the landlord did not act unreasonably. Conversely, a jury might reach an opposite conclusion. The point is that whichever conclusion is reached, it can only be done after the resolution of factual questions.

In conclusion, the appellees owed Melissa a duty, the scope of which must be determined upon a consideration of the circumstances and attendant factors in this case, and the foreseeability of harm. Whether the appellees breached their duty is a fact question. Accordingly, we reverse the summary judgment in favor of the appellees and remand this matter for further proceedings.

JOE W. CONTRERAS, Judge

CONCURRING:

J. THOMAS BROOKS, Presiding Judge

JACOBSON, Judge, dissenting:

I must again express my views as to the liability of a landlord for injuries occurring on the leased premises.[4] In my opinion, the majority in analyzing this liability confuses duty concepts associated with owners of land as compared to leaseholds and misclassifies the relationship of minor children of tenants.

Relying upon A.R.S. §33-1310(15) and *McLeod v. Newcomer*, 163 Ariz. 6, 785 P.2d 575 (App. 1989), the majority concludes that almost four-year old Melissa is a "tenant," and therefore is entitled to certain legal rights arising out of the landlord/tenant relationship. However, the statutory definition does not support this conclusion. It provides that a tenant is "a person entitled under a rental agreement to occupy a dwelling unit *to the exclusion of others.*" A.R.S. §33-1310(15) (emphasis added). Admittedly, Melissa may be entitled to occupy the premises as a child of the signatory-lessee parents, but clearly she is not entitled to do so "to the exclusion of others." There is no contention that this four-year old is liable for rent or that she would be liable for any breaches of the lease. These obligations and responsibilities go to the heart of the statutory definition and the statutory duties and obligations imposed by the code. *See generally* A.R.S. §33-1301 *et seq.* (Arizona Residential Landlord and Tenant Act).

Insofar as it can be read to imply that a landlord/tenant relationship exists for a minor child of lessee/parents, *McLeod* does so by relying upon the Ninth Circuit decision in *Schultz v. Eslick*, 788 F.2d 558 (9th Cir. 1986). *Schultz*, in turn, in attempting to forecast how Arizona would decide the issue of the duty owed by a landlord to a minor child of a tenant, relied upon cases dealing with the legal duties owed by any possessor of land to an invitee. With all due respect to the Ninth Circuit and the *McLeod* court, which held that the "landlord's duty to a tenant is analogous to that of a property owner to an invitee," 163 Ariz. at 11, 785 P.2d at 580, the duties are not analogous and the legal obligations flowing from the relationships are completely different.

In a landlord/tenant relationship, the landlord relinquishes not only possession of the premises to the tenant, but *control* of the premises as well. Thus, the tenant, not the landlord, becomes the possessor of the land. *Restatement (Second) of Torts* §356, comment (a) (1965) (*Restatement*). For example, in this case, Melissa's parents had complete control of whether the window out of which Melissa fell was to be opened or closed. It is this fundamental right to control the use of the property which passes to the tenant under a lease that distinguishes a possessor of land from that of a lessor. Therefore, both the *Schultz* and the *McLeod* analysis in describing the relationship between a landlord and a minor child of a tenant is flawed. Both cases do, however, accurately describe the legal relationship between the tenant/parent and the child.

The proper legal classification of the relationship between the parties is crucial to the proper resolution of the problem. As stated in *Shannon v. Butler Homes, Inc.*, 102 Ariz. 312, 317, 428 P.2d 990, 995 (1967), the duty of a possessor of land in so far as children are concerned "is to exercise such care as a reasonable prudent person would exercise toward children under like circumstances." This duty describes what a tenant, as possessor of the land, owes to an invitee minor (including minor children). It does not, however, describe the duty owed by a landlord to an invitee of the tenant. That duty is described in *Restatement* §356:

> Except as stated in §§357-362, a lessor of land is not liable to his lessee *or to others on the land* for physical harm caused by any dangerous condition, whether natural or artificial, which existed when the lessee took possession.

(Emphasis added.) The third-story window, if it can be classified as a dangerous condition, existed when Melissa's parents, as lessees, took possession of the premises, and therefore the landlord is not liable for physical injuries caused by that alleged dangerous condition.

Assuming that the landlord knew that the third-story window was a dangerous condition and that it involved an unreasonable risk of harm to persons, other than the tenant, then the landlord would be liable for physical injuries caused by that condition only if:

> (a) the *lessee* does not know or have reason to know of the condition or the risk involved, *and*
>
> (b) the lessor knows or has reason to know of the condition, and realizes or should realize the risk involved, and has reason to expect that the *lessee* will not discover the condition or realize the risk.

Restatement §358(1).

It is important at this juncture to identify the "lessee" referred to in the *Restatement*: it is the person with whom the owner has a legal contractual relationship, in this case, Melissa's parents. If we assume that the landlord was aware of the dangers and risks associated with the third-story window, we must likewise assume that Melissa's parents also knew of the dangers associated with the window because it was *equally obvious* to both. This is not a situation in which the open and obvious condition is a factor in determining whether the defendant was negligent, as noted by the majority. Rather, it goes to describing the legal duty owed. If, as a matter of law, the condition was obvious to any onlooker, then the landlord had no duty to protect the lessee and any other person on the premises from injuries resulting from the condition. *See Cummings v. Prater*, 95 Ariz. 20, 386 P.2d 27 (1963); *McFarland v. Kahn*, 123 Ariz. 62, 597 P.2d 544 (1979).

The majority contends that the condition insofar as it is open and obvious must be assessed from Melissa's standpoint. As has been noted, this inquiry is simply irrelevant because the landlord's duty to protect against hidden dangers refers to dangers hidden from the tenant -- Melissa's parents. It then became the obligation of those parents as possessors of the premises to take such precautions as would be taken by a reasonably prudent person.

This is not a question of transferring any obligations that the landlord owed Melissa to her parents. If liability exists in this case, it rests with Melissa's parents who opened the window to air the room, thus creating the hazard by allowing the unattended child to fall through the window. Melissa's parents should not be allowed to transfer their negligence as possessor of the property to the landlord.

I would affirm.

EINO M. JACOBSON, Judge

---

1. It is unclear from the record whether the apartment in which the bedroom window from which Melissa fell is located on the second or third story of the apartment building. For the purposes of this appeal, we assume that the apartment was in fact on the third floor of the building, as appellants assert. *See, e.g., Wagenseller v. Scottsdale Memorial Hosp.*, 147 Ariz. 370, 388, 710 P.2d 1025, 1043 (1985).

2. The general contractor moved for summary judgment on the negligence claim on the grounds that there was no evidence of negligently performed construction. The trial court, by order, granted the general contractor's motion for summary judgment. Appellants have not appealed from the trial court's order granting the general contractor's motion for summary judgment. The architect moved for summary judgment on the negligence claim and the trial court denied the motion finding that factual issues existed as to the possible negligent design of the window.

3. Appellees have objected to the inclusion of several pages of deposition testimony contained in appellants' opening brief on the grounds that these pages were not presented to the trial court and are not part of the record on appeal. Specifically, appellees object to pages 22 and 41 of Don Engler's testimony and to page 44 of Raymond Jordan's testimony. We have reviewed the record and find that page 22 of Don Engler's testimony and page 44 of Ray Jordan's testimony were not part of the record before the trial court. An appellate court's review is limited to the record before the trial court. *GM Dev. Corp. v. Community Am. Mortgage Corp.*, 165 Ariz. 1, 4, 795 P.2d 827, 831 (App. 1990); *Schaefer v. Murphey*, 131 Ariz. 295, 299, 640 P.2d 857, 861 (1982). Accordingly, we will not consider the pages of deposition testimony not before the trial court in the proceedings below.

4. *Udy v. Calvery Corp.*, 162 Ariz. 7, 780 P.2d 1055 (App. 1989) (Jacobson, J., specially concurring).

J. Stanley Edwards
EDWARDS & EDWARDS
11000 North Scottsdale Road
Suite No. 135
Scottsdale, Arizona 85254
(602) 991-1938
State Bar No. 004190

Attorneys for Plaintif

IN THE SUPERIOR COURT OF THE STATE OF ARIZONA

IN AND FOR THE COUNTY OF MARICOPA

MARC A. , a single man, Plaintiff, vs. BERNADETTE M. and JOHN DOE husband and wife, Defendants.	No. CV 90-31964 PLAINTIFF'S SETTLEMENT CONFERENCE MEMORANDUM (Conference Set for February 21, 1992 at 10:30 A. M.) (Assigned to the Hon.

Plaintiff, Marc A. hereinafter referred to as "Marc", by and through counsel undersigned, hereby submits his Pretrial Settlement Conference Memorandum pursuant to this Court's Minute Entry of November 5, 1991.

I. **STATEMENT OF PLAINTIFF'S CLAIM.**

Marc was injured in an automobile accident on January 20, 1989, when Defendants' vehicle executed a left-hand turn in front of Marc's 1989 Mercury causing a collision to occur near the intersection of 19th Avenue and Bell Road in Phoenix, Arizona.

After the accident Marc was taken to the emergency room of Humana Desert Valley Hospital and subsequently sought care with an

EDWARDS & EDWARDS
Attorneys at Law
11000 North Scottsdale Road, Suite 135
Scottsdale, Arizona 85254
(602)991-1938

orthopaedic physician, Dr. Anthony T. a chiropractor, Dr. Albert D. C.; Dr. Lynne D. O., and Dr. Brad L. M. D., an orthoapedic surgeon. After non-evasive treatment was attempted and was unsuccessful, Dr. performed an arthroscopy of Marc's left knee.

To date, Marc's medical expenses since the accident of January 20, 1989, total approximately $14,000.00. Complicating the situation is a second accident in August of 1989. It did not involve Marc's left knee, but resulted in additional treatment by Dr. Dr. has allocated $2,000.00 of the total medical expenses incurred by Marc with her to the second accident.

Marc was discharged from his employer, , Inc., in November of 1989. Marc alleges that his frequent absences from work were due to the accident and having to seek medical treatment was the primary cause of his termination of employment. Marc sustained a wage loss of approximately $2,000.00 during the period from January of 1989 until his discharge in November and was not able to obtain meaningful employment thereafter until October of 1990. At the time of Marc's discharge, he was earning approximately $290.00 per week with , Inc., and his lost-wage claim from November of 1989 until he obtained meaningful employment in October of 1990 would be approximately $12,500.00.

II. **STATEMENT OF DEFENDANTS' CLAIM**.

Marc believes that Defendants will not dispute responsibility for the accident but will deny that the accident was the legal cause for all of Marc's injuries. It is believed that

EDWARDS & EDWARDS
Attorneys at Law
11000 North Scottsdale Road, Suite 135
Scottsdale, Arizona 85254
(602)991-1938

Defendants will also allege that Marc's discharge from Inc., in 1989 was unrelated to the accident of January 20, 1989. It is also believed that Defendants will allege that contrary to Marc's statement at the time of the accident, that Marc was not wearing appropriate restraints and Defendants may therefore allege that the injuries were more serious than they would otherwise have been. It is further believed that Defendants will allege that the injuries sustained by Marc to his knee were not caused by the accident but were rather the result of a pre-existing condition.

III. PLAINTIFF'S POSITION AND SUMMARY OF THE EVIDENCE.

(1) Marc will submit medical records showing that he suffered a bruise on his knee at the time of the accident and that subsequently developed serious symptoms with regard to that knee. He will also testify that he was wearing a seatbelt at the time of the accident and that his knee was asymptomatic prior to the accident. His treating physicians, Dr. and Dr. have both expressed opinions relating his knee problems to the accident of January 20, 1989, and the reasonableness of their treatment of him and the necessity for surgery. Dr. who treated Marc for approximately three months after the accident, will also testify as to the reasonableness of the charges and the necessity for the chiropractice services provided.

(2) Marc will submit medical records establishing that the medical expenses were, in fact, incurred and that extensive damage was done to the vehicle that he was driving. Indeed, the damage to the vehicle was so extensive the car was totaled.

EDWARDS & EDWARDS
Attorneys at Law
11000 North Scottsdale Road, Suite 135
Scottsdale, Arizona 85254
(602)991-1938

(3) Marc will also submit his employment records establishing his lost wages during the period from January, 1989 to November, 1989, and will testify with respect to his attempts to obtain employment from November of 1989 until October of 1990.

IV. DEFENDANTS' POSITION AND SUMMARY OF EVIDENCE.

Defendants' position regarding Marc's claim has been previously set forth. It is believed that Defendants will introduce the Independent Medical Examination Report of Dr.
regarding his examination of Marc in January of 1992. It is further believed that Defendants may utilize a video tape recording taken of Marc while working at his place of employment. Defendants have not at this time listed any witnesses in an attempt to establish their "seatbelt" defense or any witnesses who would attempt to establish that, in fact, Marc was not wearing his seatbelt at the time of the accident.

V. SUMMARY OF SETTLEMENT NEGOTIATIONS.

Plaintiff originally filed an Offer of Judgment for $90,000.00. Defendants then filed an Offer of Judgment in the amount of $27,500.00. Plaintiff thereafter filed an Offer of Judgment in the amount of $61,000.00. The timeframe for accepting any of the Offers of Judgment submitted has expired.

Other than the Offers of Judgment filed herein, no substantive negotiations regarding settlement have been undertaken by the parties.

VI. ANTICIPATED RESULTS IF THE CASE PROCEEDS TO TRIAL.

Plaintiff is confident that if this case proceeds to trial

EDWARDS & EDWARDS
Attorneys at Law
11000 North Scottsdale Road, Suite 135
Scottsdale, Arizona 85254
(602)991-1938

a jury verdict in favor of Plaintiff is inevitable. The amount of any verdict would be dependent upon the jury's findings regarding Marc's lost-wage claim of $2,000.00 pre-termination and $12,500.00 post-termination. Should the jury determine that Marc's termination was not accident related, Plaintiff would expect a jury verdict in the $50,000.00 to $75,000.00 range. Should the jury determine that Marc's termination was causally related to his accident, Plaintiff would expect a jury verdict in the range of $60,000.00 to $85,000.00.

RESPECTFULLY SUBMITTED this 18th day of February, 1992.

EDWARDS & EDWARDS

By ______________________
J. Stanley Edwards
11000 North Scottsdale Road
Suite No. 135
Scottsdale, Arizona 85254
Attorneys for Plaintiff

EDWARDS & EDWARDS
Attorneys at Law
11000 North Scottsdale Road, Suite 135
Scottsdale, Arizona 85254
(602)991-1938

COPY of the foregoing
mailed/faxed this
18th day of February, 1992,
to:

Phoenix, Arizona 85014
Attorneys for Defendants

Judge of the Superior Court
Maricopa County Superior Court
East Courts Building
101 West Jefferson Street
Phoenix, Arizona 85003

ORIGINAL of the foregoing
delivered this 18th day

of February, 1992, to:

Clerk of the Superior Court
Central Courts Building
201 West Jefferson Street
Phoenix, Arizona 85003

J. Stanley Edwards

EDWARDS & EDWARDS
Attorneys at Law
11000 North Scottsdale Road, Suite 135
Scottsdale, Arizona 85254
(602)991-1938

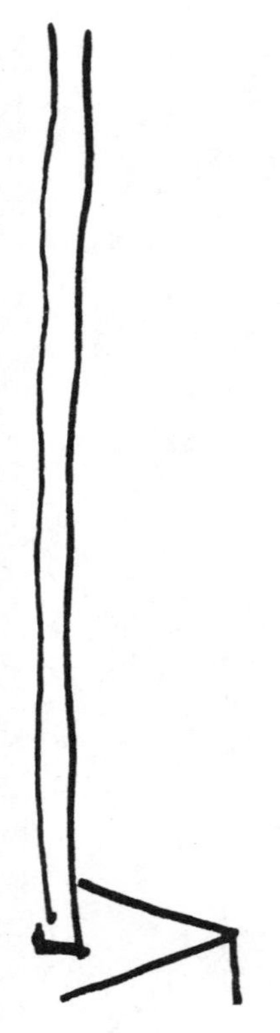

Boy, We Sure got Lucky with that Attempted Monkey Break-out!! ... You growing A beard, Phil?!

STUDY GUIDE
CHAPTER FOUR

1. If two people come in for an interview and you determine that your firm may have a conflict of interest if you were to represent them both, what should you do? (43)

2. At what point should you tell a potential client that you are a legal assistant? (44)

3. What kinds of information should you get from a potential client during an initial interview? (44)

4. Is the attorney-client privilege applicable to conversations between a client and a legal assistant? (44)

(a) Is the privilege applicable to conversations that take place at an initial interview if the firm declines to represent an individual? (44)

5. What should you try to accomplish at the initial stages of an interview? (44)

(a) How might you accomplish these things? (44)

6. How should you phrase your questions at the beginning of an interview with a potential client, i.e., should you ask directed or open-ended questions? (45)

7. What are the benefits of using notes and prepared questions during an interview? (45)

(a) What is the possible problem with using notes and prepared questions? (45)

8. What should you pay attention to other than an interviewee's actual words when he/she is speaking? (45)

9. Why is it important to summarize what you believe an interviewee has said to you? (45)

10. What kinds of human relations skills are helpful in conducting interviews? (45)

(a) Is it true that you should detach yourself as much as possible during an interview? (45-46)

11. In what sense is interviewing a two-way street? (46)

12. What kind of background information must you gather in any personal injury suit? (46-47)

13. After an interviewee describes events to you what should you do? (47-48)

14. Why might an attorney decide not to accept a personal injury case? (48)

15. Why is it important that you discover discrepancies in an interviewee's story during the initial interview? (48)

(a) Should you assume any information relayed to you by an interviewee is truthful and accurate? (48)

16. What might your firm do if the statute of limitations was about to expire shortly after you first met a potential client? (49)

17. Is the investigation of a traffic accident necessarily conducted by a police officer? (49)

18. Why is it important to interview a police officer as soon after an incident occurs as possible? (49)

19. How should you go about contacting a police officer you wish to interview? (49)

20. What are some things to keep in mind when interviewing a police officer if you want to ensure optimum cooperation? (50)

21. Other than determining what an officer observed firsthand what kinds of information should you obtain from an officer? (50)

22. What are the reasons for and against tape recording an interview with a lay witness? (51)

23. What should you tell a lay witness before you begin your questioning? (51)

24. Should you discourage a witness from talking to opposing counsel? (51)

25. Why should you try to pinpoint the exact location of a witness at the time he/she was observing events critical to your case? (51)

26. Why should you try to pin down a hostile witness to specific details? (52)

27. Should you allow a witness to review the transcript of his/her interview? (52)

28. What valuable information other than personal firsthand information can a witness provide? (52)

REVIEW QUESTIONS

1. What should you do and say at the beginning of an interview to set the stage?

2. How should you structure an interview? What kinds of questions should you ask? Should you use notes?

3. What kinds of information should you get during an initial interview of a potential client? What kinds of observations should you make?

4. What should you consider in preparing for an interview with a police officer?

5. What kinds of information should you try to get from a police officer? From a witness?

6. What should you consider when deciding whether to tape record an interview?

7. How should you deal with a hostile witness?

PUTTING IT INTO PRACTICE

Read the scenario described at the beginning of Chapter Five. Assume that your firm represents Teddy and that you have been assigned to interview Jonathan. His parents are reluctant to allow him to talk with you since they are very close friends of the Baxters and want to avoid doing anything that might jeopardize their friendship. What might you do to get Jonathan to open up to you? How would you deal with his parents?

The following pages represent a sample of the documents used in filing a lawsuit and the instructions given to the process server to have the documents served.

FILING AND SERVICE INSTRUCTIONS

To: MICHAEL J. FLEMING
& ASSOCIATES
Process Service

Attorney: J. Stanley Edwards
Phone: 991-1938
Secretary: Julie

Date: ______________________

Name of Court ____

Case No. ____________________________________
Name of Case ____
____

Documents Attached: ____
____
____
____
____
____

Fee Attached: ____

Instructions for Filing: ____________________________________
____
____
____
____

Instructions for Delivery: __________________________________
____
____
____
____

Service/Additional Instructions: ____________________________
____
____
____
____
____
____
____

Name of Person or Corporation to be Served		
Address(es) for Service		
Firm or Attorneys		
Date	Phone	
Type of Papers		
Remarks		
File #	Case #	

Process Service
Instruction Form

PLEASE COMPLETE

PLEASE TYPE ALL INSTRUCTIONS

To our clients: Accurate information is essential if we are to give you quick and efficient service. This instruction sheet will be returned to your office with the receipt and cause number. We must ask you to complete and submit this form with all papers given to us for service. For our mutual protection and to avoid any future misunderstandings, we will not accept any papers for service without this form. Please note that a separate form should be completed for each Defendant, with the exception of married couples residing at the same address.

MICHAEL J. FLEMING — PRIVATE PROCESS SERVICE
STATEWIDE SERVICE
COURT MESSENGER SERVICE
P. O. Box 3882, Phoenix, AZ 85030 Phone 253-1165

J. STANLEY EDWARDS
11000 N. Scottsdale Road, Suite 135
Scottsdale, Arizona
991-1938
State Bar No. 004190
Attorney for Plaintiff

In The Superior Court Of The State Of Arizona
In And For The County Of Maricopa

CIVIL COVER SHEET

____
CASE NUMBER

Pursuant to Rule 3.1 (a) Superior Court Local Rules - Maricopa County, please provide the following information. *(Type or print)*

PLAINTIFF'S NAME

List additional plaintiffs on reverse side

PLAINTIFF'S ATTORNEY

____
Name and State Bar Number

DEFENDANT'S NAME(S)

List additional defendants on reverse side.

PLAINTIFF'S ADDRESS(ES)

CASE PREFERENCE

____
Cite Statute or Rule

AMOUNT IN CONTROVERSY (If alleged)
Compensatory $ ______________
Punitive $ ______________
Attorney Fees $ ______________

EMERGENCY ORDER SOUGHT:
______ TRO
______ Provisional Remedy
______ Other ______________
Specify

REASON FEES NOT PAID:
☐ Governmental Charge
☐ Deferred

LOCATION:
Southeast Judicial District
Yes ☐ No ☐

NATURE OF ACTION

Place an "X" next to the one which describes the nature of the case.
If more than one, circle the predominant one.

100 TORT MOTOR VEHICLE
____ 101 Non Dealth Injuries
____ 102 Property Damage
____ 103 Death

110 TORT NON-MOTOR VEHICLE
____ 111 Negligence
____ 112 Products Liability
____ 113 Intentional
____ 114 Property Damage
____ 115 Legal Malpractice
____ 116 Other ______________
Specify

120 MEDICAL MALPRACTICE
____ 121 Physician-M.D.
____ 122 Physician-D.O.
____ 123 Hospital
____ 124 Other ______________
Specify

130 CONTRACTS
____ 131 Account (Open or Stated)
____ 133 Foreclosure
____ 134 Other ______________
Specify

140 APPEAL OR REVIEW

- ____ 141 Civil Traffic
- ____ 142 Civil Non-Traffic
- ____ 143 Tax
- ____ 144 Administrative Review
- ____ 145 Special Action

150-170 OTHER CIVIL

- ____ 151 Forcible Detainer
- ____ 152 Change of Name
- ____ 153 Transcript of Judgment
- ____ 154 Foreign Judgment
- ____ 155 Declaratory Judgment
- ____ 156 Eminent Domain
- ____ 157 Habeas Corpus
- ____ 158 Quiet Title
- ____ 159 Restoration of Civil Rights
- ____ 160 Seized Vehicle
- ____ 161 DES Instant Judgment
- ____ 162 Harassment
- ____ 163 Other ________________________ Specify

To the best of my knowledge, all information is true and correct.

____
Attorney's Signature

ADDITIONAL PLAINTIFF(S)

ADDITIONAL DEFENDANT(S)

NOTICE

Effective July 1, 1987 and pursuant to Superior Court (Maricopa County) Local Rule 3.1 (a), the Superior Court requests that a "Cover Sheet", which categorizes the cause of action, accompany any new action filed with the Superior Court in Maricopa County. For this purpose, the form on the reverse side has been developed. The cover sheet will result in increased accuracy of court records and statistics, and in reduced processing time for new case filings.

Forms will be made available at the Clerk of the Superior Court's Filing Counter.

PLEASE DO NOT INCLUDE THIS FORM WITH CASES WHICH HAVE ALREADY BEEN FILED. This form can only be processed **at the time of filing** New Complaints and Petitions.

Thank you for assisting us with our efforts to improve service.

STUDY GUIDE
CHAPTER FIVE

1. How is negligence defined? (59)

   (a) How does negligence compare to an intentional tort? (59)

2. What are the four elements of neligence? (59)
   (a)

   (b)

   (c)

   (d)

3. How is the nature of one's duty determined? (59-60)

   (a) What is the key question involved in determining whether a defendant breached his/her duty? (60)

4. What is the difference between an objective and a subjective standard? (60)

5. Are the physical characteristics of a tortfeasor taken into consideration in deciding the reasonableness of conduct? (61)

6. To what standard of care are professionals held? (61)

7. What is negligence per se? (61)

(a) When might negligence per se be applicable? (61)

8. What is the doctrine of res ipsa loquitur? (61)

(a) What are the elements of this doctrine? (61-62)

(1)

(2)

(3)

(b) Under what circumstances might a plaintiff want to rely on this doctrine? (62)

9. What is the difference between actual cause and proximate cause? (62)

10. In what type of situations is actual cause a problem to prove? (62)

11. What does the issue of proximate cause revolve around? (62)

12. What is the "eggshell skull" rule? (62)

13. What is an unforeseeable plaintiff? (63)

(a) How did that issue arise in Palsgraf? (63)

14. What is the relationship between duty and proximate cause? (63)

15. What is the purpose of compensatory damages? (64)

(a) What are the two categories of compensatory damages and what is the difference between the two? (64)

(1)

(2)

16. What is the difference between compensatory, nominal and punitive damages? (63-64)

17. Can nominal damages be awarded in a negligence case? (64)

18. In what types of cases are punitive damages awarded? (64)

19. What is the difference between the role of a jury and the role of a judge? (65)

20. For what reasons might a judge remove a case from a jury? (64)

21. What is the difference between the burden of production and the burden of persuasion? (65)

(a) What are the consequences of failing to meet the burden of production? (65)

(b) How does <u>res ipsa loquitur</u> affect the plaintiff's burden of proof? (65)

(c) How might one quantify the plaintiff's burden of persuasion? (65)

REVIEW QUESTIONS

1. What are the key issues involved under duty and breach of duty?

2. How do the concepts of negligence per se and res ipsa loquitur assist a plaintiff?

3. For a plaintiff what problems can arise in regard to the element of causation?

4. Identify the types of damages a plaintiff might recover after being injured by a defective product.

PUTTING IT INTO PRACTICE

Suppose your firm's client, an insurance salesman, is injured when he falls over a roller skate left lying on the sidewalk of his customer's house. He wants to sue his customer for negligence. What will he have to prove to recover? Consider each element of negligence and what kinds of evidence will have to be presented. If, on the other hand, your firm represents the insurance carrier of the customer what will you want to argue in order to get a directed verdict?

KEY TERMS

Define the following:

Actual cause

Breach of duty

Burden of persuasion

Burden of production

Compensatory damages

General damages

Negligence *per se*

Nominal damages

Objective standard

Proximate cause

Punitive damages

Res ipsa loquitur

Special damages

Subjective standard

The following is a sample offer of judgment filed by the plaintiff along with the notice of filing docketed with the clerk of the court. Check to see if your state allows a plaintiff to file an offer of judgment.

J. Stanley Edwards
EDWARDS & EDWARDS
10505 North 69th Street
Suite No. 800
Scottsdale, Arizona 85253
(602) 991-1938
State Bar No. 004190

Attorneys for Plaintif

Edwards & Edwards
Attorneys at Law
10505 North 69th Street, Suite 800 • Scottsdale, Arizona 85253 • (602) 991-1938

IN THE SUPERIOR COURT OF THE STATE OF ARIZONA

IN AND FOR THE COUNTY OF MARICOPA

MARC A. , a single man, Plaintiff, vs. BERNADETTE M. and JOHN DOE husband and wife, Defendants.	No. CV 90- PLAINTIFF'S NOTICE OF OFFER OF JUDGMENT

To: Defendants, and their attorneys of record, Garrey & Curran, P. C., and the Clerk of the Court:

NOTICE IS HEREBY GIVEN that, pursuant to Rule 68, Arizona Rules of Civ.Proc., as revised, Plaintiff has served an Offer of Judgment upon the Defendants this date to be accepted in writing within thirty (30) days after serevice hereof. This Notice is filed in lieu of the original Offer of Judgment.

DATED this 26 day of September, 1991.

EDWARDS & EDWARDS

By

J. Stanley Edwards
10505 North 69th Street
Suite No. 800
Scottsdale, Arizona 85253
Attorneys for Plaintiff

COPY of the foregoing
mailed/delivered this
26 day of September, 1991,
to:

Suite No. 230
Phoenix, Arizona 85014
Attorneys for Defendants

J. Stanley Edwards

Edwards & Edwards
Attorneys at Law
10505 North 69th Street, Suite 800 • Scottsdale, Arizona 85253 • (602) 991-1938

Res Ipsa
Loquiter !!
BANG
BANG
WAAAAAAAA
WAAAAAAAA
AAAOOOOOOOOO

STUDY GUIDE
CHAPTER SIX

1. In general terms what is the duty of a defendant? (72-73)

2. Was the common law designed to protect landowners or possessors? (73)

(a) What was the purpose behind that protection? (73)

3. To what duty of care was a possessor held under the common law? (73)

(a) Have all states retained the common law classification when determining the duties owed by a possessor? (73)

4. What duty of care does a possessor owe a trespasser? (73-74)

(a) What are the four exceptions to that rule? (74)
(1)

(2)

(3)

(4)

5. What are the five elements of the attractive nuisance doctrine? (74-75)

(a)

(b)

(c)

(d)

(e)

6. Is the age, experience and intelligence of a child taken into consideration in the attractive nuisance doctrine? (75)

7. In what way is the difference between natural conditions and artificial conditions taken into consideration for purposes of this doctrine? (76)

8. Does the attractive nuisance doctrine in essence require a possessor to make his/her land child-proof?

9. What is the "rescue" or "danger invites rescue" doctrine? (76)

(a) How does this doctrine protect plaintiffs? (76)

(b) When is this doctrine inapplicable? (76)

10. When does a possessor owe a duty of care to a known trespasser? (76)

(a) What is the rationale behind this rule? (76)

11. What is the rule regarding trespassers who use only a limited portion of the possessor's land? (77)

12. What is a licensee? (77)

(a) What duty of care is owed to a licensee? (77)

(b) Is there any duty to inspect for dangers? (77)

13. What is an invitee? (77)

(a) Is someone who is not doing business with the possessor at the time he/she is injured still considered an invitee? (77)

(b) Can a social guest rise to the level of invitee by performing services for the host? (78)

14. How does one lose one's invitee status? (78)

15. What duty of care is owed an invitee? (78)

(a) How does one determine what "reasonable care" is? (78-79)

(b) Does the posting of warning signs always constitute "reasonable care"? (79)

16. Do all states distinguish between trespassers, licensees and invitees? (79)

17. What duty is owed to those injured outside of one's property? (79)

(a) How is that duty affected by whether the condition is artificial or natural? (80)

18. Under the common law do individuals have any duty to assist those with whom they have no special relationship? (80)

(a) Does it matter that they could assist and incur no harm to themselves? (80)

19. Give some examples of special relationships that create a duty of care? (80)

20. Give an example of a situation in which a duty of care arises because of a special relationship between the defendant and a third party. (81)

(a) Does a university have any duty to protect its students from harm? (81)

21. How does Tarasoff affect professionals? (81)

22. Can tavern owners and social hosts be held liable for the acts of intoxicated persons to whom they provide liquor? (82)

23. What duty of care is owed to one to whom you administer emergency assistance? (82)

(a) What is the reasoning behind this rule? (82)

24. To whom did the common law give the most protection - tenants or landlords? (83)

(a) Why? (83)

25. What are the duties of a tenant? (83)

26. What duties does a landlord retain even though he/she transfers possession to a tenant? (83)

(a) Is a landlord's failure to keep the premises in good repair if he/she contracts to do so considered tortious conduct? (83)

(1) If yes, what must a tenant prove? (83)

(b) What is the duty of landlords once they begin making repairs, even if they are not contractually obligated to do so? (83)

(c) Does a landlord have a duty to take security precautions? (see arguments raised in Kline) (83)

27. Do sellers of land retain any liability once they turn property over to the buyers? (91-92)

(a) If yes, what duties do they have? (92)

28. Under the common law could a child recover for injuries sustained while a fetus? (92)

(a) Has that rule changed today? If so, how? (92)

29. What is the doctrine of vicarious liability? (92)

30. What is the doctrine of "respondeat superior"? (92)

(a) When is this doctrine applicable? (92)

(b) What is the rationale behind this doctrine? (93)

31. What is the "family purpose" doctrine? (93)

REVIEW QUESTIONS

1. What are the duties of care a possessor of land owes to others?

2. What special relationships create a duty of care?

3. What duties arise out of the landlord-tenant relationship and the buyer-seller relationship?

4. Give some examples of vicarious liability.

PUTTING IT INTO PRACTICE

One of your firm's clients owns a rather large Arabian horse breeding farm. One day a young girl is thrown while riding one of the client's horses and is badly hurt. Your client wants to know if he can be sued. What kinds of questions would you ask in order to answer his question? Would it matter if your client was on the premises at the time of the injury?

KEY TERMS

Define the following:

Attractive nuisance

Family purpose doctrine

Invitee

Licensee

Rescue doctrine

Respondeat superior doctrine

Vicarious liability

The following pages represent a sample document used during discovery.

J. Stanley Edwards
EDWARDS & EDWARDS
10505 North 69th Street
Suite No. 800
Scottsdale, Arizona 85253
991-1938
State Bar No. 004190

Attorneys for Plaintiff

IN THE SUPERIOR COURT OF THE STATE OF ARIZONA

IN AND FOR THE COUNTY OF MARICOPA

MARC A. a single man, Plaintiff, vs. GEORGE F. and CHERYL husband and wife, Defendants.	No. CV 91- NOTICE OF SERVICE OF DISCOVERY PAPERS

Pursuant to Superior Court Local Rules of Maricopa County, the undersigned party has served certain Discovery Papers upon the opposing counsel (and opposing parties who have appeared for themselves without counsel), if any, whose names and addresses where served are listed below:

Phoenix, Arizona 85080-2330
Attorneys for Defendants

The Discovery Papers that were served with a copy of this Notice are described below:

Plaintiff's Answers to Defendants' Uniform Interrogatories.

Unless otherwise indicated above, all papers were served by mailing through the United States Mail on the below date.

DATED: November ____, 1991.

EDWARDS & EDWARDS

By ________________________________
J. Stanley Edwards
10505 North 69th Street
Suite No. 800
Scottsdale, Arizona 85253
Attorneys for Plaintiff

STUDY GUIDE
CHAPTER SEVEN

1. At what moment in time is the reasonableness of a defendant's conduct evaluated? (98)

2. What question was Judge Learned Hand attempting to answer through the use of his formula? (99)

3. What is the Learned Hand formula? (100)

(a) Summarize the meaning of his formula. (99-100)

(b) What do the courts look at in considering the burden of precautions? (100)

(c) Use this formula to argue that a reasonable car manufacturer should include an air bag in the design of its cars. (100-101)

4. How does the Restatement position compare with the Learned Hand formula? (101)

5. What is the difference between an objective and a subjective standard? (101-102)

(a) Why is the objective standard usually used in tort law? (102)

6. Does the law take into account a person's mental stability in determining the reasonableness of his/her conduct? (102)

(a) What about a person's IQ? (102)

7. To what standard is an intoxicated person held? (102-103)

8. To what standard are insane people held? (103)

(a) What is the reason for adhering to such a standard? (103)

9. Does the law take into account the physical attributes of an individual? (103)

(a) Give an example. (103)

(b) How are unknown physical conditions treated? (103)

10. To what standard of care are children held? (103)

(a) When are they held to an adult standard of care? (103)

11. To what standard of care is one held in an emergency? (104)

(a) In what, if any, circumstances might a person be expected to anticipate the actions of others? (106)

12. How is custom used in determining the reasonable standard of care? (107)

(a) Does adherence to custom necessarily preclude a defendant from being found negligent? (107)

13. To what standard of care is a professional held? (107)

(a) What is the difference in standard of care for a general practitioner and a neurosurgeon? (107)

(b) Is a novice in a profession held to a lower standard of care than a more experienced individual? (107)

14. What is negligence <u>per</u> <u>se</u>? (107)

(a) What are the elements of negligence <u>per</u> <u>se</u>? (107)

15. In what way is negligence per se problematic when it comes to cases involving the stealing of cars? (108)

16. Does the violation of a criminal statute necessarily result in civil liability? (108)

(a) What is the majority rule? (108)

17. Are there ever circumstances in which the violation of a statute will be considered negligence per se even though the defendant acted reasonably? (108)

(a) Give an example. (108)

18. How do different jurisdictions treat the violation of a statute (if the statutes do not impose an absolute duty of compliance)? (108-109)

19. Are contributory negligence and assumption of risk viable defenses in cases of negligence per se? (109)

20. If a defendant acts in compliance with a statute is he/she presumed not to be negligent? (109)

21. What is an automobile guest statute? (109)

22. What is the doctrine of res ipsa loquitur? (109)

(a) What four things must a plaintiff prove? (109-110)
(1)

(2)

(3)

(4)

23. If it is just as likely that someone other than the defendant caused the plaintiff's injuries, does the doctrine of res ipsa loquitur apply? (110)

24. Why does the plaintiff often have a difficult time proving negligence when there are multiple defendants? (110)

(a) Why do some courts allow plaintiffs to rely on res ipsa loquitur in such cases? (110)

25. Is a plaintiff required to prove that only negligence could have been the cause of the injuries he/she sustained? (110-111)

26. Is the doctrine applicable if the plaintiff was contributorily negligent? (111)

27. Is the doctrine applicable if the evidence of negligence is just as available to the plaintiff as it is to the defendant? (111)

28. What are the procedural consequences of relying on the doctrine of res ipsa loquitur? (111)

REVIEW QUESTIONS

1. What general rules have been established to determine the reasonableness of a defendant's conduct?

2. In what way has the law attempted to objectively assess the reasonableness of conduct (e.g., using formulas or guidelines)?

3. Explain how a plaintiff can use the doctrines of negligence _per se_ and _res ipsa loquitur_ to help prove her case.
   (a) What might a defendant argue in response to the use of these doctrines?

PUTTING IT INTO PRACTICE

A client asks your firm to represent her in a medical malpractice claim against a gynecologist that uses both traditional (allopathic) and holistic approaches to treating her patients. The client says she had emergency surgery that saved her life but resulted (she claims) in a recurring pain in her left leg. She never experienced such pain before and nothing she or any physician does alleviates this constant pain. She also says that after the surgery the gynecologist used some non-traditional techniques, which were designed to expedite the healing process. How will you go about determining whether the doctor breached her duty of care?

KEY TERMS

Define the following:

Learned Hand formula

Negligence _per se_

Res ipsa loquitur

The following is a sample offer of judgment filed by defendant.

Phoenix, Arizona 85014
(602)

State Bar No.

Attorneys for Defendants

IN THE SUPERIOR COURT OF THE STATE OF ARIZONA

IN AND FOR THE COUNTY OF MARICOPA

MARC A. a single man, Plaintiff, vs. BERNADETTE M and JOHN DOE husband and wife, Defendants.	NO. CV 90- DEFENDANTS' NOTICE OF OFFER OF JUDGMENT

To: Plaintiffs, and their attorney of record, J. Stanley Edwards, and the Clerk of the Court

NOTICE IS HEREBY GIVEN that, pursuant to Rule 68, Arizona Rules of Civil Procedure, as revised, Defendants have served an Offer of Judgment upon the Plaintiff this date to be accepted in writing within thirty (30) days after service hereof. THIS NOTICE is filed in lieu of the original Offer of Judgment in order to prevent unnecessary duplication of the pleadings in this Court's file.

. . . .

. . . .

. . . .

. . . .

. . . .

DATED this 15th day of July, 1991.

By ____________________

Suite 230
Phoenix, AZ 85014
Attorneys for Defendants

COPY of the foregoing
mailed this 15th day
of July, 1991,
to:

J. Stanley Edwards, Esq.
Edwards & Edwards
10505 North 69th Street
Suite 800
Scottsdale, Arizona 85253

____

Phoenix, Arizona 85014
(602)

State Bar No.

Attorneys for Defendants

IN THE SUPERIOR COURT OF THE STATE OF ARIZONA

IN AND FOR THE COUNTY OF MARICOPA

MARC A. a single man, Plaintiff, v. BERNADETTE M. and JOHN DOE husband and wife, Defendants.	No. CV 90- **OFFER OF JUDGMENT**

To: Plaintiffs and their attorneys of record:

The Defendants, pursuant to Rule 68, Arizona Rules of Civil Procedure, as revised, hereby offer to allow the Plaintiff to take judgment against them in the above-entitled action for the sum of TWENTY-SEVEN THOUSAND FIVE HUNDRED DOLLARS AND NO/100 ($25,500.00). If this offer is not accepted in writing within thirty (30) days after service hereof, it shall be deemed withdrawn.

. . . .

. . . .

. . . .

. . . .

. . . .

. . . .

DATED this 18th day of July, 1991.

By [signature]

Phoenix, Arizona 85014
(602)
Attorneys for Defendants

Original and one copy of the foregoing mailed this 18th day of July, 1991, to:

J. Stanley Edwards, Esq.
Edwards & Edwards
10505 N. 69th Street
Suite 800
Scottsdale, Arizona 85253
Attorneys for Plaintiffs

By [signature]

STUDY GUIDE
CHAPTER EIGHT

1. Is actual causation a factual or policy question? (118)

2. What is the "but for" test? (118-119)

   (a) In what way is this test very broad? (119)

3. What is the "substantial factor" test? (119)

4. How do successive events differ from concurrent ones? (119)

   (a) If two independent tortfeasors act successively to cause a harm to occur, are they both considered the actual cause of the harm? (119)

5. Who bears the burden of proving actual causation? (120)

   (a) What if the defendant argues that the plaintiff would have been injured even if the defendant had not been negligent? (120)

6. What is the theory of alternate liability? (120)

7. How does the theory of market share liability differ from alternate liability? (120)

(a) Illustrate how this theory could be used in a product liability case. (120)

(b) How does the market share liability theory differ from res ipsa loquitur? (121)

8. What is the concerted action theory? (121)

9. What is the judicial policy underlying "proximate" or "legal" cause? (121)

10. What is the fundamental question that proximate cause deals with? (121)

11. Summarize the facts of Palsgraf. (122)

(a) What was the central question in this case? (122)

(b) What was the court's reasoning? (129)

(c) What is the Cardozo rule? (129-130)

(d) How does Andrews' dissent differ from the majority? (130)

(e) Which is generally followed today - the Cardozo or Andrews position? (130)

12. What is direct causation? (130)

(a) How does it compare to Andrews' dissent? (130)

(b) What is a common criticism of direct causation? (130)

(c) What is a response to that criticism? (130)

13. What is the relationship between duty and proximate cause? (130)

14. What is the "eggshell skull" rule? (131)

15. What is the rule regarding proximate cause if the harm that occurs is of the same general type that made the defendant's conduct negligent but occurs in an unusual manner? (131)

(a) Make up your own example of this principle.

16. What is the rule regarding proximate cause if the plaintiff is not a particularly foreseeable plaintiff? (131)

(a) Make up your own example of this principle.

17. What is an intervening cause? (132)

(a) When does an intervening cause become a superseding cause? (132)

(b) Does a defendant remain liable if there are intervening causes? (132)

(c) Does a defendant remain liable if there are superseding causes? (132)

18. Give an example of an intervening cause. (132)

(a) Is the negligence of rescuers (such as paramedics) a superseding cause? (132)

(b) Is medical malpractice a superseding cause? (133)

(c) Is the criminal conduct of a third person considered a superseding cause? (133)

19. For what reason are tavern owners not exempted from liabliity when the guests they serve injure others? (133)

20. Give an example of a superseding cause. (133)

21. Is an unforeseeable intervention a superseding cause if it leads to the same type of harm as that threatened by the defendant's negligence? (133-134)

(a) Why not? (134)

22. Is the issue of proximate cause a jury question or a question for the judge? (134)

REVIEW QUESTIONS

1. Describe how a plaintiff might go about proving actual causation when several defendants are involved in causing his/her injuries.

2. Describe the two basic positions adopted by the courts in determining proximate cause.

3. In what types of cases do the courts take exception to the majority position regarding proximate cause?

4. When does an intervening cause become a superseding cause?

PUTTING IT INTO PRACTICE

A client is severely injured in an automobile accident, as a result of which she suffers from chronic fatigue and excruciating migraine headaches, among other maladies. She did on occasion before the accident complain of migraines but they never occurred with the frequency or intensity they do now. She claims that her treating physician was negligent in his care of her and is suing him as well. The defendant doctor claims that she failed to follow his instructions and that she used remedies that were in conflict with the treatment program he had recommended. What actual cause and proximate cause issues does this situation present?

KEY TERMS

Define the following:

But-for test

Eggshell skull rule

Intervening cause

Substantial factor test

Superseding cause

The following pages represent sample interrogatories and answers. The first set represents interrogatories prepared by defendant's attorney. The second set represents uniform interrogatories approved for use in the state of Arizona.

Phoenix, Arizona 85080-2330
(602)
Direct Line:
Attorneys for Defendants

IN THE SUPERIOR COURT OF THE STATE OF ARIZONA

IN AND FOR THE COUNTY OF MARICOPA

MARC A. a single man, Plaintiff, v. GEORGE F. and JANE DOE husband and wife, Defendants.	NO. CV 91- **NONUNIFORM INTERROGATORIES TO PLAINTIFF**

TO: Plaintiff, MARC A. , and J. STANLEY EDWARDS, his attorney.

Under authority of Rule 33, Arizona Rules of Civil Procedure, Defendant(s) hereby request(s) that the above plaintiff answer the following Interrogatories in writing and under oath, within thirty (30) days from the receipt hereof.

DEFINITIONS AND INSTRUCTIONS

1. When used in these Interrogatories, where appropriate, the word "plaintiff", or "you", or "your" includes, if necessary, any and all plaintiff(s) and in addition, concerning anything that relates to or is relevant to the issues of this litigation, plaintiff's counsel and any agent, servant, employee, representative, private investigator, or any other person who has acted for or who has obtained information for or on behalf of plaintiff(s).

2. When used in these Interrogatories, the word "defendant" includes, if necessary, the defendant(s) propounding these Interrogatories, and in addition, where appropriate, concerning any matter that relates to or is relevant to the issues in this litigation, counsel for such defendant(s) and any agent, servant, employee, representative, private investigator, or other person who has acted for or who has obtained information for or on behalf of any such defendant propounding these Interrogatories.

3. "Incident", unless specifically said to the contrary, means any one of, or any number of, or all of the liability events described in the Complaint.

4. If you are asked to identify a person, please state for each person:

(a) the person's full name;

(b) the person's spouse, if any;

(c) the person's last known home address and telephone number;

(d) the person's last known business address and telephone number;

(e) the person's employer at the time referred to in the particular Interrogatory that asks for the person's identity.

5. If you are asked to identify a non-person (e.g., a corporation, partnership, etc.) state:

(a) the name;

(b) the type of entity it is;

(c) its business address at the time referred to in the Interrogatory inquiry;

(d) if different than in the answer to (c) above, its present business address.

6. If you are asked to identify a document, provide the following:

(a) its date;

(b) identification of each person who prepared it;

(c) a general description of its type, kind or sort;

(d) its subject matter;

(e) identification of each custodian.

7. Whenever the singular form is used in these Interrogatories, where appropriate, it is intended to apply additionally to the plural form.

8. Whenever the plural form is used in these Interrogatories, where appropriate, it is intended to apply additionally to the singular form.

9. When used in these Interrogatories, the word "complaint" refers to any complaint or third-part claim or cross-claim that you are making against the defendant(s) propounding these Interrogatories.

10. When used in these Interrogatories, the word "witness" refers to any person, lay or expert (except an attorney who does not have personal or testimonial knowledge), including you, who has information concerning any issue in this litigation, regardless of whether the party answering these Interrogatories expects or intends to present the testimony of such person at trial.

11. Supplementation of responses to these Interrogatories is demanded in accordance with Civil Rule 26(e), A.R.S. 1956.

BACKGROUND AND INFORMATION

1. State your full name.

2. State your social security number.

3. State your present age and your birth date.

4. State your height, weight, color of eyes and hair.

5. If you are presently married, state the name of your spouse and the date of your marriage.

6. If you have previously been married, state the name of each spouse, the date of the consummation of each marriage and if terminated, the date and whether it was terminated by separation, annulment, divorce or death.

7. If you have plans to be married or you are engaged, state to whom, approximately when and where.

8. If you have any children, state the name and age of each child, whether the child is living with you or elsewhere, and if elsewhere, state the address. If any child is married, state the name of such child's spouse.

9. What is your present address?

10. What was your address at the time of the incident which gave rise to this lawsuit?

11. Other than the addresses mentioned in Interrogatories 9 and 10, state each and every address wherein you have resided from ten (10) years before the incident which gave rise to this lawsuit to the present time, and state the approximate dates of each residence.

12. With whom did you reside at the time of the incident which gave rise to this lawsuit?

13. Have you ever been examined for life insurance?

If so, state what insurance company, the approximate date, and the name and address of the examining physician.

14. Have you ever been refused any life insurance?

If so, by what company, when, for what reason, and state the name and address of the examining physician.

15. During the past ten (10) years, have you been a member of any social club, lodge or association? If so, state the name and address of each such organization and the period of time and dates of each such association.

16. During the past ten (10) years, have you participated in any hobby?

If so, as to each hobby, state it and the dates of the participation.

17. List all forms of recreation, including but not limited to physical or sports recreation, in which you have participated during the past ten (10) years.

18. Have you ever served in the Armed Forces or performed services for any branch of any governmental agency?

If your answer is in the affirmative, please state: (a) the name of each such organization and particular branch for whom you performed services; (b) the dates and places of performance of such services; (c) the serial or identification number you had; (d) a detailed description of the services performed; (e) whether or not a physical examination was required and if so, the dates and places of such examinations and your best recollection of the findings of such examination; (f) the date of termination of service in each instance; and (g) a detailed description of the reasons why the services were terminated.

19. Have you ever been or are you a party to a lawsuit other than this present litigation and other than mentioned elsewhere in these answers?

If so, as to each action, state: (a) what party you were; (b) identify and state the party status of the other parties; (c) identify the court where such action was filed and state the court file number of such action; (d) identify the attorneys representing the respective parties and state which party each attorney represented; (e) describe the basic issues and contentions of the various parties; (f) state how such issues and contentions were decided, and (g) if a judgment was rendered or entered, state what it provided.

20. Have you ever been charged, indicted, convicted or imprisoned for any felony?

If so, please state the date and place of each such incident, the charge and the ultimate disposition of each such incident.

21. Have you ever been charged, indicted, convicted or imprisoned for any misdemeanor resulting in a jail sentence or in probation?

If so, please state the date and place of each such incident, the charge and the ultimate disposition of each such incident.

PRE-EXISTING PHYSICAL OR MENTAL CONDITION

22. Have you ever suffered or do you suffer from fainting spells, blackouts, fits or epilepsy? If so, please describe in detail.

23. Have you ever suffered or do you suffer from diabetes, tuberculosis, malaria or venereal disease? If so, describe in detail.

24. Prior to the incident described in the complaint, did you have any physical condition that restricted the movement of any part of your body?

If so, describe in detail.

25. Have you ever been confined or treated for alcoholism or for drug abuse?

If so, describe in detail.

26. Prior to the incident described in the complaint, have you ever suffered from any mental illness or nervous disorder?

If so, state: (a) the date of the commencement of such occurrence; (b) a detailed description of the condition and its symptoms; (c) the cause of such condition; (d) the duration of such condition; (e) describe the treatment received, and (f) identify all persons, organizations or institutions rendering treatment or where you received treatment.

27. Since the incident described in the complaint (other than because of injuries you relate to such incident), have you suffered from any mental illness or nervous disorder?

If so, answer the questions asked in the second paragraph of the preceding Interrogatory.

28. If you have received medical care or treatment during the five (5) years immediately preceding the incident which gave rise to this lawsuit: (a) identify all persons, organizations or institutions rendering treatment or where you received treatment; (b) state the date or dates of care or treatment; (c) describe the symptoms that caused the care or treatment; (d) describe your care and treatment; and (e) describe the medical condition you believe you had.

29. If you have received medical care or treatment since the incident described in the complaint (other than for injuries you relate to such incident), answer all of the questions in the preceding Interrogatory.

30. Other than stated elsewhere in your answers to these Interrogatories, have you ever had any illness, sickness or disease other than minor colds, viruses or childhood ailments?

If so, as to each condition, state the following: (a) the date or dates of the condition; (b) your symptoms; (c) identify all persons, organizations or institutions rendering treatment or where you received treatment; (d) if you have recovered, the approximate date of your recovery; and (e) if you have not recovered fully, state your symptoms at the time of the incident described in the complaint and at the present time.

31. Other than stated elsewhere in your answers to these Interrogatories and except for birth, have you ever been hospitalized?

If so, as to each hospitalization, state the following: (a) identify the hospital; (b) the dates of admission and discharge; (c) identify each medical practitioner who treated you; (d) the physical or mental condition necessitating the hospitalization; and (e) the treatment you received.

32. Other than the incident described in the complaint, have you ever suffered any injuries in any accident, automobile or otherwise, that required more than 3 medical treatments or which resulted in a permanent injury? If so, as to each accident, state: (a) the date and place of the accident; (b) a detailed description of all the injuries you received; (c) identify all persons, organizations or institutions rendering treatment or where you received treatment; (d) whether you have recovered from the injuries; (e) if you have recovered from the injuries, the date you recovered; (f) if you have not recovered from the injuries, describe your symptoms at the time of the incident described in the complaint and at the present time; (g) whether you made a claim for damages arising out of the accident, and if you did, provide the following information: (1) identify the person or organization that you claimed was responsible for your injuries; (2) identify any insurer of the person or organization described in (1) above; (3) whether you were compensated and if so, the amount you received and the date you received such; (4) whether you

retained an attorney and if you did, identify the attorney; (5) whether a lawsuit was filed and if it was, answer all the questions asked in Interrogatory 19.

33. Do you claim any aggravation of a pre-existing condition as a result of the injuries you claim to have sustained in the incident described in the complaint?

If so, describe in detail.

LOSS OF EARNINGS AND EARNING CAPACITY

34. Do you claim to have sustained a loss of earnings or earning capacity as a result of the incident described in the complaint?

If the answer is no, it is not necessary to answer Interrogatories 35 through 46.

35. Have you had any special training or education for any type of employment or work?

If so, describe.

36. Were you employed or self-employed at the time of the incident described in the complaint?

If so, (a) identify your employer; (b) identify your immediate supervisor; (c) describe your duties; (d) state the dates of such employment; (e) state you r rate of pay at the time of the incident described in the complaint and (1) state the basis of such pay, e.g., a regular salary with or without overtime or a commission or both; (2) what this rate of pay was for each month of the six (6) months immediately preceding the incident described in the complaint.

37. Are you employed or self-employed at the present time?

If so, and your employment is the same as at the time referred to in Interrogatory 36 but changes have occurred since the incident as to information contained in the answer to Interrogatory 36, state the changes.

If your employment since the incident described in the complaint has been or is different than at the time referred to in Interrogatory 36, answer as to each employment the questions set forth in Interrogatory 36.

38. Have you ever been employed or self-employed other than as referred to above?

If so, as to each such employment or self-employment from ten (10) years preceding the incident described in the complaint to the present time, answer each of the questions asked in Interrogatory 36.

39. As to loss of earnings you claim to have resulted from the incident described in the complaint, state: (a) the condition(s) that you believe caused you to incur the loss of earnings; (b) the amount of your loss of earnings to date; (c) the dates during which you claim to have suffered complete loss of earnings and the amount lost during said time; (d) the dates during which you claim the loss of earnings was partial and the amount lost during said time; (e) the specific manner in which the amount of the loss of earnings was determined; (f) whether you received any unemployment insurance for such loss of earnings and if so, state the time, the amount received, and identify the person or organization that paid such loss.

40. For how many years prior to the present year do you have copies of your income tax returns to the United States government?

41. If you filed an income tax return for any of the ten (10) years immediately preceding the incident described in

the complaint, as to each such year state where the return was filed.

42. For each of the ten (10) years immediately preceding the incident described in the complaint: (a) identify each person or organization from whom you received income; (b) state the amount of income you received; and (c) state how much of each source of income was reported on your appropriate United States income tax return.

43. Answer the questions of Interrogatory 42 as to income during the year in which the incident described in the complaint occurred.

44. For any full or partial years after the year during which the incident described in the complaint happened to the present time, answer the questions set forth in Interrogatory 42.

45. Identify each of the high schools, colleges or educational institutions you have attended, and list the dates of attendance, courses of study, and the degree attained, if any.

46. Other than stated in the answer to Interrogatory 45, if you have received any special education or training for any type of work, state: (a) its nature; (b) if the training or education was at a training or educational institutions, identify it and state the dates of attendance; (c) if the training or education was on-the-job training, identify the employer, state the dates of the training and describe in detail its nature.

INJURIES AND NON-LOSS OF EARNING DAMAGE CLAIMED TO HAVE RESULTED FROM INCIDENT AT ISSUE

47. Describe in detail what happened to you physically during and immediately after the incident described in the complaint and include what parts of your body, if any, came in contact with what.

48. State in your own words what personal injuries, if any, you received as a result of the incident described in the complaint.

49. Have you suffered any pain in connection with the injuries you claim to have received in the incident described in the complaint?

If so, as to each different pain: (a) describe it; (b) state whether it is still existent; (c) if it is not still existent, state when it ceased; (d) if it is still existent, state the course of such pain in intensity from its origin to the present time; (e) if it is still existent, state (1) whether it waxes or wanes; (2) what activities, if any, cause it to become more severe; (3) what, if anything, causes any relief or diminishment of such pain; (f) if such pain has caused any incapacitation, describe the amount of incapacitation and when it occurred; (g) if not answered above, describe any restriction in activities such pain has caused and when.

50. Have you been hospitalized as a result of the incident described in the complaint?

If so, as to each hospitalization, identify the hospital, identify the doctor who admitted you, identify each other doctor who treated or cared for you, state the date of your admission and discharge, state how you were taken to the hospital, state the treatment you received and the amount of the hospital bill.

51. Have you received any out-patient or emergency treatment from any hospital as a result of the incident described in the complaint?

If so, as to each treatment, state the date of the treatment, the charge and what was done.

52. What doctors or other medical practitioners have treated you for injuries you claim to have received as a result of the incident described in the complaint? As to each doctor or medical practitioner, state the following: (a) identify the doctor or medical practitioner; (b) if the doctor or medical practitioner is a specialist, state each specialty; (c) identify each person who recommended that you consult such doctor or medical practitioner; (d) state the nature and extent of the treatment you received; (e) state the date or dates of each treatment; (f) state the amount you have been charged to date by such doctor or medical practitioner; (g) state whether any of such charges have been paid and if so, identify each person or organization that made any payment and state when; (h) state the place of each of your treatments; (i) state whether any doctor or medical practitioner prescribed that you take any medicine and if so, describe each medicine, state each date it was taken and why you believe it was prescribed; (j) state each complaint of pain or injury you have made to such doctor or medical practitioner.

53. Do you have any scheduled appointments in the future for medical treatment for the injuries you claim to have sustained in the incident described in the complaint?

If so, identify the person, organization or institution where the treatment is scheduled and state when and for what complaints or symptoms.

54. Have any doctors or medical practitioners recommended to you that you incur any future medical expenses or undergo any future medical treatment as a result of the injuries you claim to have sustained because of the incident described in the complaint?

If so, as to each treatment, to the best of your knowledge identify the person, organization or institution who will render treatment or where the treatment will be received, state why you believe it will be rendered or received, state the approximately date of such treatment and state the approximate expected charges for such treatment.

55. Has any doctor or medical practitioner told you that you would be permanently disabled because of injuries you relate to the incident described in the complaint?

If so, identify such doctor or medical practitioner, state in substance what said doctor or practitioner said to you and state when such was said.

56. Has any doctor or medical practitioner told you that you will suffer pain and/or discomfort in the future because of injuries you relate to the incident described in the complaint?

If so, answer the questions asked in the second paragraph of the preceding interrogatory.

57. Other than already set forth in your answers to these interrogatories, have you incurred any medical expense which you claim to have been the result of the incident described in the complaint?

If so, as to each expense state when it was incurred, its nature, the amount charged, whether it has been paid, and if paid, when and who paid it.

58. Other than previously mentioned in the preceding interrogatories, have you sustained any item of damage which you claim to have been incurred as a result of the incident described in the complaint?

If so, please explain each item of damage fully, its amount, when the expense was incurred and the reason that you claim such item to be the result of the incident described in the complaint.

59. As to any future damages you believe you will incur as a result of the incident described in the complaint that have not already been described in the answers to these interrogatories: (a) describe the damage; (b) state the amount of damage you expect you will incur in the future; (c) state the reason for such damage; and (d) identify the person or organization, if any, to whom you expect to be indebted.

60. Have you ever received to the present time or are you receiving benefits because of any Workmen's Compensation Act, or a similar Act, or any disability pension of any type or nature whatsoever or benefits because of any insurance?

If so, as to each benefit: (a) identify the person or organization which paid the benefit; (b) state the date and the amount of the payment; (c) describe the medical condition and your symptoms which caused payment of the benefits.

61. From the date of the incident described in the complaint, have you participated in any hobby or hobbies or any form of recreation, including but not limited to physical or

sports recreation, that you did not participate in prior to the accident in question?

If so, please explain fully.

62. From the date of the incident described in the complaint to the present time, have you had a physical or mental examination for any purpose other than previously stated in the answers to these Interrogatories?

If so, as to each examination, identify the person or organization who performed the examination, state its date and the reason for such examination.

DISCOVERY AND INVESTIGATION

63. Are you aware of any statement made at the scene of the incident described in the complaint by any person (including you or any part or any other person)?

If so, as to each separate statement, (a) identify the person making the statement, (b) identify all persons present within hearing distance when the statement was made, (c) identify each person to whom the statement was made,

J. Stanley Edwards
EDWARDS & EDWARDS
10505 North 69th Street
Suite No. 800
Scottsdale, Arizona 85253
991-1938
State Bar No. 004190

Attorneys for Plaintiff

IN THE SUPERIOR COURT OF THE STATE OF ARIZONA

IN AND FOR THE COUNTY OF MARICOPA

MARC A. a single man, Plaintiff, vs. GEORGE F. and CHERYL husband and wife, Defendants.	No. CV 91- PLAINTIFF'S ANSWERS TO DEFENDANTS' UNIFORM INTERROGATORIES

I am a party in this civil action or an officer or agent of a party upon whom the attached Interrogatories were served. Pursuant to RCP 33, I have answered them separately and fully in writing or have stated an objection in lien of an answer. The answers and objections to the Interrogatories are set forth in the space below each Interrogatory. All answers and objections are attached to this Response.

I have read the attached Answers to Interrogatories and know of my own knowledge that the facts stated therein are true and correct and swear to the foregoing.

Marc A. , Affiant

STATE OF ARIZONA)
) ss.
County of Maricopa)

The foregoing was acknowledged before me, the undersigned Notary Public, this _____ day of November, 1991, by MARC A.

My commission expires: ______________________________
Notary Public

ATTORNEY'S CERTIFICATION

Any objections to Interrogatories are made by me on behalf of the named party. I have served upon the propounding party and all other parties or their attorneys, as evidenced by the Mailing Certificate attached hereto, either a copy or the original and one copy of this Response pursuant to the Rules of Practice of the Superior Court.

DATED this _____ day of November, 1991.

EDWARDS & EDWARDS

By ______________________________
J. Stanley Edwards
10505 North 69th Street
Suite No. 800
Scottsdale, Arizona 85253
Attorneys for Plaintiff

GENERAL BACKGROUND AND INDENTIFICATION

501. (a) State your full name.

Marc Alan

(b) State any and all other names which you have ever used or by which you have been known.

None.

502. State each and every address which you have had in the last five years, including your present address, and the dates of your residence at each.

West Saharo Drive, Phoenix, Arizona; North 77th Drive, Phoenix, Ariozna 85033; East Rosemonte, Phoenix, Arizona 85024 (present address).

503. State the date and place of your birth.

February 14, 1969; Greenfield, Massachusetts.

504. (a) Which of the following is your present marital status: single, married, separated, widowed or divorced.

Singe.

(b) State the name and last-known address of your spouse and every former spouse.

Not applicable.

(c) State the date and place of each such marriage.

Not applicable.

(d) As to previous marriage, please give the date, place and manner of each termination.

Not applicable.

(e) State the name, age and address of each of your children.

Michael R. , five years old; East Rosemonte, Phoenix, Arizona 85024.

505. State your height in feet and inches.

5' 10".

506. State your weight in pounds.

180 pounds.

507. State the color of your eyes.

Hazel.

508. State the color of your hair.

Brown.

509. State your Social Security Number.

510. (a) Have you ever been a party to a civil lawsuit? Yes.

If so, state:

(b) Were you plaintiff or defendant?

Plaintiff.

(c) What was the nature of the plaintiff's claim?

Tort - Motor Vehicle. Claim for personal injuries and lost wages.

(d) When, where and in what court was the action commenced?

The action was commenced in the Maricopa County Superior Court, Arizona, on November 26, 1990.

(e) State the names of all parties other than yourself.

The parties to the action are Bernadette and Charles Defendants.

511. (a) Have you ever been convicted of a felony? No.

If so, state:

Not applicable.

(b) What was the original charge made against you?

Not applicable.

(c) What was the charge of which you were convicted?

Not applicable.

(d) Did you plead guilty to the charge, or were you convicted after trial?

Not applicable.

(e) What was the name and address of the court where the proceedings took place?

Not applicable.

512. State the highest grade of formal schooling completed by you and any certificates or degrees received.

12th Grade; high school diploma.

513. (a) Have you ever served in the Armed Forces of the United States? No.

If so, state:

(b) The branch of service.

Not applicable.

(c) Your serial number.

Not applicable.

(d) The date of commencement and termination of service.

Not applicable.

(e) The highest rank attained.

Not applicable.

(f) The type of discharge received.

Not applicable.

AUTOMOBILE ACCIDENTS: VEHICLES AND DRIVERS

521. State the date, time and place of the accident in question.

August 14, 1989 at approximately 3:15 P. M.

522. With respect to the vehicle you occupied at the time of the accident, state:

(a) The name of the driver.

Marc A.

(b) The address of the driver.

East Rosemonte, Phoenix, Arizona 85024.

(c) The name of the registered owner.

Marc A.

(d) The address of the registered owner.

East Rosemonte, Phoenix, Arizona 85024.

(e) The make, model and type of vehicle.

1989 Kawasaki motorcycle, Model No.

(f) The damage, in detail, to the vehicle.

Damage was sustained to the tail cover, lower cowl, left-hand cowl, tail lens and rear fender.

(f) The name and address of each person or organization repairing the vehicle and the cost of repairs.

Kawasaki, Phoenix, Arizona.

523. (a) Do you have information indicating, or any reason to believe, that there was any defect or failure on the part of any vehicle or equipment involved in the accident? No.

If so, state:

Not applicable.

(b) The vehicle or equipment involved.

Not applicable.

(c) The nature of the defect or failure.

Not applicable.

(d) When you first became aware of the defect or failure.

Not applicable.

(e) When and where the defect or failure was repaired or corrected.

Not applicable.

524. As to each vehicle involved in the accident, state:

(a) The number of occupants in each vehicle.

Plaintiff's motorcycle: one

Defendants' vehicle: one.

(b) The names and addresses of the occupants of each vehicle.

(1) Plaintiff, address previously supplied;

(2) Defendant, George F. West Phelps Road, Phoenix, Arizona 85023.

(c) The position of each occupant in each vehicle.

(1) Plaintiff was the driver of his motorcycle;

(2) George F. was the driver of his 1984 Ford van.

525. If you were driving or operating one of the vehicles involved in the accident:

(a) Did you have a license, permit or certificate issued by any governmental authority to operate a motor vehicle? Yes.

If so, state:

(b) The type thereof.

Chauffeur's license.

(c) The governmental authority issuing it.

State of Arizona.

(d) The number which it bears.

No.

(e) The date of issuance and date of expiration.

February, 1985; May 7, 1993.

(f) The nature of any restrictions placed thereon.

None.

526. If you were driving one of the vheicles involved in the

accident:

(a) Did you receive a citation for violating any statute or ordinance as a result of the accident or of the events leading up to said accident? No.

If so, state:

(b) The specific statute or ordinance you were charged with having violated.

Not applicable.

(c) The governmental authority issuing the citation.

Not applicable.

(d) Whether you pled guilty to the charge made in the citation.

Not applicable.

527. (a) In the 24-hour period immediately preceding the accident, did you consume any alcoholic beverage or take a sedative, tranquilizer or other drug or medicine? No.

If so, state:

(b) What was consumed.

Not applicable.

(c) When it was consumed.

Not applicable.

(d) Where it was consumed.

Not applicable.

(e) The name and addresses of all persons present at the time of consumption.

Not applicable.

528. (a) At the time of the accident, did you suffer from any physical or mental condition which could have impaired, influenced or affected your ability to operate or mannoer of operating a motor vehicle? No.

If so, state:

(b) The name or type of condition.

Not applicable.

(c) The date of the onset of the condition.

Not applicable.

(d) The name and address of each medical practitioner who ever treated you for the condition.

Not applicable.

DESCRIPTION OF ACCIDENT AND INVESTIGATION

531. How did the accident occur?

Plaintiff was going to work at Revlon, Inc., when he stopped at a traffic light at 43rd Avenue and Van Buren Street and was hit in the rear of his motorcycle by Defendants' 1984 Ford van.

532. Where were you coming from at the time of the accident?

Plaintiff was coming from his residence.

533. Where were you going at the time of the accident?

Plaintiff was going to his place of employment at Revlon, Inc.

534. Describe the route you followed from the point where your trip commenced to the place where the accident occurred.

Plaintiff had left his residence at East Rosemonte, Phoenix, Arizona 85024 and was headed Southbound on I-17 to Van Buren Street and was heading Westbound on Van Buren Street to Revlon, Inc., at the time the accident occurred.

535. (a) Are you aware of any person who may have or claims to have knowledge of the accident, any of the events leading up to it or related events occurring thereafter? Yes.

If so, state:

(b) The name of each such person.

(1) Defendant, George F. Brunton.

(2) Officer D. , Phoenix Police Department, the officer who investigated the accident initially.

(c) The last-known address of each such person and your means of ascertaining the present whereabouts of each person.

(1) Address previously supplied.

(2) 620 West Washington Street, Phoenix, Arizona 85003.

(d) The occupation and employer of each person.

(1) Unknown.

(2) Police officer with the Phoenix Police Department.

536. (a) Are you aware of the existence of any written or recorded statement made by any party or witness? No Accident Report of which Plaintiff is aware was prepared with respect to the accident.

If so, state:

(b) The name of each person making the statement.

Not applicable.

(c) The date of the statement.

Not applicable.

(d) The name, employer, occupation and last-known address of the person or persons taking the statement.

Not applicable.

(e) The name and last-known address of the person now in possession of the original statement.

Not applicable.

537. (a) Where any photographs or motion pictures taken of the accident scene or of any object or person involved in the accident? None of which Plaintiff is aware.

If so, state:

(b) What is depicted by each photograph and/or motion picture.

Not applicable.

(c) The date on which each film or picture was taken.

Not applicable.

(d) The name and address of the photographer.

Not applicable.

(e) The name and address of the person who now has custody of the photographs or pictures.

Not applicable.

538. (a) Have any drawings, plats or diagrams of the scene of the accident, or of any object involved in the accident which you intend to use upon the trial of this case been prepared since the time of the accident? No.

If so, state:

(b) What is depicted in each drawing, plat or diagram.

Not applicable.

(c) When each item was prepared.

Not applicable.

(d) The name and address of the person who prepared each item.

Not applicable.

539. (a) Were any tests, inspections or measurements made or taken with respect to the accident scene or any object involved? None of which Plaintiff is aware.

If so, state:

(b) The subject of each test, inspection or measurement.

Not applicale.

(c) The name and address of the person who conducted each test, inspection or measurement.

Not applicable.

(d) The date on which each test, inspection or measurement was performed.

Not applicable.

(e) The name and address of the person now having custody of any written report concerning each test, inspection or measurement.

Not applicable.

540. (a) Was an investigation conducted concerning the accident in question? None other than the initial investigation by Officer McElvain after the accident.

If so, state:

(b) The name, address and occupation of the person who conducted each investigation.

See Answer to previous Interrogatories.

(c) The name and address of the person who requested each investigation to be made.

(d) The date on which each investigation was conducted.

(e) The places where each investigation was performed.

(f) The name and address of the person now having custody of each written report made concerning each investigation.

541. (a) Do you know of any person who is skilled in any particular field or science whom you may call as a witness at the time of trial of this case and who has expressed an opinion upon any issue of this action? Yes.

If so, state:

(b) The name and address of each person.

Plaintiff intends to call as witnesses at trial of this case his treating physicians. The names and addresses of such medical providers have been previously provided to Defendants pursuant to their Request for Production of Documents.

(c) The field or science in which each such person is sufficiently skilled to enable him to express opinion evidence in this action.

Plaintiff's treating physicians are all qualified and sufficiently skilled in medicine to enable them to give opinions with respect to treatment of Plaintiff's injuries.

(d) Whether such potential witness will base his opinion:

(1) In whole or in part upon facts acquired personally by him in the course of an investigation or examination of any of the issues of this case or,

Plaintiff's treating physicians will base their opinions on their own examination and treatment of Plaintiff's injuries as well as any reports and medical records they may have examined from Plaintiff's other medical providers.

(2) Solely upon information as to facts provided to him by others.

See Answer to (d)(1) above.

(e) If your answer to Interrogatory No. 541(d) discloses that any such witness has made a personal investigation or examination relating to any of the issues of this case, state the nature and dates of such investigation or examination.

See copies of Plaintiff's medical records from his treating physicians previously made available to Defendants.

(f) Each and every fact and each and every document, item, photograph or other tangible object supplied or made available to such person.

See Answers to previous Interrogatories.

(g) The general subject upon which each such person may express an opinion.

See Answers to previous Interrogatories.

(h) Whether such persons have rendered written reports.

If so:

(1) Give the dates of each report.

See copies of Plaintiff's medical records previously provided to Defendants.

(2) State the names and addresses of the custodian of such reports.

Copies of Plaintiff's medical records are in the possession of Plaintiff's attorney and attorneys for Defendants.

INJURIES AND DAMAGES

551. State the name of each person for whom you claim damages for personal injuries.

Plaintiff, Marc A.

552. Describe in detail all injuries and symptoms, whether physical, mental or emotional, experienced since the occurrence and claimed to have been caused, aggravated or otherwise contributed to by it.

Plaintiff sustained injuries to his back, neck, head and left knee. He suffers from headaches, back and neck pain and the muscles in his back and eyes are subject to spasms. He subsequently lost his job because of the amount of time he had to take off from work.

553. As to each medical provider who has examined or treated any of the persons named in your answer to Interrogatory No. 551 above, for any of the injuries or symptoms described, state:

(a) The name, address and specialty of each medical provider.

See copies of Plaintiff's medical records previously provided to Defendants.

(b) The date of each examination or treatment.

See copies of Plaintiff's medical records previously provided to Defendants.

(c) The physical, mental or emotional condition for which each examination or treatment was performed.

See copies of Plaintiff's medical records previously provided to Defendants.

554. Has any person named in your answers to Interrogatory No. 551, been hospitalized since the occurrence? Yes.

If so, state:

(a) The name and location of each hospital in which each was confined.

Humana Hospital - Desert Valley, Emergency room.

(b) The dates of each hospitalization.

(1) August 14, 1989;
(2) June 22, 1990.

(c) The conditions treated during each hospitalization.

(1) Neckaches and headaches.
(2) Plaintiff was assaulted and hit in the head with a rock.

(d) The nature of the treatment rendered during each hospitalization.

(1) Soft-collar was applied and medication prescribed.
(2) Sutures were made of the laceration and Plaintiff was treated for a bite on his left cheek.

555. (a) Have any diagnostic studies, tests or procedures been performed since the accident? Yes. See copies of Plaintiff's medical records previously provided to Defendants.

If so, state:

(b) The nature thereof.

Acute cervical strain;

(c) The name, address and occupation of the person performing same.

Dr. E. Humana Hospital - Desert Valley, 3929 East Bell Road, Phoenix, Arizona 85032;

(d) The place where performed, and if in a clinic, laboratory or hospital, the name and address thereof.

See Answer to No. 555(a) above.

(e) The name and present or last-known address of each party now in possession or control of any records prepared in connection with each study, test or procedure.

Plaintiff's counsel and Defendants' counsel.

556. (a) Is any person named in your answer to Interrogatory No. 551 still under the care of any medical practitioner? Yes.

If so, state:

(b) The name and address of each practitioner.

Dr. Brad L. , M. D.; address previously supplied;

(c) The nature of each condition for which care is being rendered.

Injury to knee;

(d) Which of the conditions are related to the accident?

Not applicable.

557. State as to each item of medical expense attributable to the accident:

(a) The amount.

$1,434.15. See copies of Plaintiff's medical records and letter of Dr. dated February 5, 1991.

(b) The name and address of the person or organization paid or owed therefor.

Dr. Lynne , D. O., North Phoenix Health Institute. See information previously supplied.

Dr. Albert Chiropractic Clinic; address previously supplied;

(c) The date of each item of expense (attach copies of itemized bills, if desired).

See copies of Plaintiff's medical records.

PRE-EXISTING AND AGGRAVATED INJURIES

561. List each injury symptom or complaint mentioned in answer to Interrogatory No. 552 from which you suffered at any time before the accident.

Plaintiff was involved in an automobile accident on January 20, 1989, in which he sustained injuries to his back, neck, head and left knee. He suffers from headaches, back and neck pain and the muscles in his back and eyes are subject to spasms and his knee is often sore and painful. He was forced to have knee surgery as a result of the accident and subsequently lost his job because of the amount of time he had to take off from work. The accident in which he was involved on August 14, 1989, aggravated and worsened his physical condition and has caused the healing process to be considerably slowed.

562. (a) Are any of the injuries or conditions which you claim were caused by the accident an aggravation or a pre-existing condition? Yes.

If so, state:

(b) Which of the injuries or conditions are aggravations or pre-existing conditions?

Plaintiff's treating physicians have indicated that Plaintiff had a pre-existing condition with his left knee. See Answer to No. 561 above.

(c) What were the pre-existing conditions?

Plaintiff's physicians had previously informed him (prior to this accident that he had a pre-existing condition in his left knee known as Osgood Schlatlers disease. The Osgood Schlatlers disease became symptomatic as a result of the January 20, 1989 accident.

(d) The name and address of each medical practitioner who treated the pre-existing condition.

Dr. Brad L. , M. D.; Dr. Lynne , D. O.; Dr. Albert

D. C.; Dr. Anthony T. M. D., East Myrtle, Suite No. 400, Phoenix, Arizona 85020.

(1) The dates of such treatments.

See copies of Plaintiff's medical records.

(2) The nature of such treatments.

See copies of Plaintiff's medical records.

563. (a) State the name and address of each medical practitioner who examined or treated you for any mental or physical condition during the five-year period immediately before the date of the accident.

Dr. Eric M. D., North 32nd Street, Suite No. A-4, Phoenix, Arizona 85028.

As to each such person, state:

(b) The conditions or complaints for which the examination or treatment was performed.

Plaintiff saw and was treated by Dr. for normal childhoold illnesses, flu and sore throats.

(c) The date of each examination or treatment performed.

Plaintiff does not recall the exact dates of the various treatments performed by Dr. but Plaintiff's counsel has requested that Plaintiff's medical records for the past five years be provided to him. Copies of the medical records will be made available to Defendants as soon as they are received by Plaintiff's counsel. Plaintiff signed and attached the Medical Authorization Release form provided by Defendants in their Request for Production of Documents in order that Defendants might receive copies of any medical records they might desire.

(d) Whether or not the symptoms evidencing the conditions described in your answer to paragraph (b) of this Interrogatory were completely relieved and, if so, the date of relief.

See Answer to No. 563(c) above.

564. (a) Were you hospitalized or confined to an institution for any physical or mental condition at any time during the ten-year period immediately before the accident? Yes. See copies of Plaintiff's medical records and Answers to previous Interrogatories.

If so, state:

(b) The name and address of each such hospital or institution.

See previous Answers.

(c) The conditions or complaints for which you were hospitalized or confined.

See previous Answers.

(d) The dates during which you were hospitalized or confined.

See previous Answers.

(e) The treatment received by you during your hospitalization or confinement.

See previous Answers.

(f) Whether or not the symptoms evidencing the conditions for which you were hospitalized were relieved, and if so, the date of relief.

See previous Answers.

565. (a) Have you had a physical examination by a medical practitioner within five (5) years prior to the accident? Yes.

If so, state:

(b) The date of the examination.

The exact date is unknown but Plaintiff believes that he was examined in order to participate in high school activities. It is also possible he may been seen by the family physician, Dr.

(c) The name and address of the medical practitioner.

Any school physician is unknown to Plaintiff. Dr. address has been previously made available.

(d) The reason for the examination.

See Answer to Interrogatory No. 565(b).

IMPAIRMENT TO EMPLOYMENT AND ACTIVITIES

571. List each job or position of employment, including self-employment, held by you on the date of and since the accident, stating as to each, the following:

(a) Name and address of employer.

But For You Saying
'ISN'T that Puppy cute';
AND Her Saying 'Please';
AND You both taking me home
... I'd Never have chewed
those really neat Perry Ellis
shoes of Yours!!

STUDY GUIDE
CHAPTER NINE

1. What are the two categories of compensatory damages? (141)

(a) For what damages do general damages compensate a plaintiff? (141)

(1) Give an example. (141)

(b) For what damages do special damages compensate a plaintiff? (141)

(1) Give an example. (141)

(c) Which of these damages must be specifically pleaded in a complaint?

2. What is the purpose of punitive damages? (141)

3. In what situations are nominal damages awarded? (141)

(a) Why can't nominal damages be awarded in negligence cases? (141)

4. What is the problem in awarding damages for pain and suffering? (143)

(a) What is the "per diem" technique and how does it objectify the process of awarding damages? (143)

(b) Why has this technique been prohibited by some courts? (143)

(c) What is the argument advanced to support the contention that damages should be awarded for pain and suffering even if such damages are highly subjective?

(d) What questions do Peck's studies raise in reference to the awarding of damages for pain and suffering? (144)

5. What are the two types of damages that fall under the category of impaired earning capacity? (145)

(a) What is the potential problem in computing past earnings? (145)

(b) What must be considered in computing a plaintiff's future lost earnings? (145)

6. What is the reasoning underlying the rule preventing plaintiffs from seeking recovery for shortened life expectancy? (145)

7. What is the collateral source rule? (145)

(a) What is the rationale for this rule? (145)

(b) Is evidence of collateral benefits admissible? (146)

8. Is the winning party entitled to recover for attorney's fees in a personal injury suit? (146)

9. For what reasons has the contingency fee arrangement been criticized? (146)

(a) What is the response to that criticism? (146)

10. How are damages computed if property is destroyed? (146)

(a) What if the property is damaged but not destroyed? (146)

(b) What if the property was neither destroyed nor damaged but the plaintiff was denied use of the property? (146)

11. What is the fair market value of property? (146)

(a) How is it computed? (146)

12. In negligence cases when can punitive damages be awarded? (147)

(a) Can they be awarded in cases involving intentional torts? (147)

(b) For what reasons is the awarding of punitive damages criticized? (147)

(c) What are some of the reasons that justify the imposition of punitive damages? (147)

(d) What are the particular problems that arise in the context of product liability cases? (147)

(e) What is the Restatement position regarding the assessment of punitive damages against employers? (147)

13. What arguments did Ford raise regarding punitive damages in the Pinto case? (147-148)

(a) What was the court's reponse? (148)

(b) What factors did the court indicate should be considered in deciding whether punitive damages are excessive? (148)

(1)

(2)

(3)

(4)

14. What losses are included under loss of consortium? (148)

(a) Why is a loss of consortium claim considered a derivative claim? (148)

(b) Under the early common law why couldn't a wife recover for loss of consortium? (148)

(c) Has that changed today? (148)

(d) Is there a potential for double recovery if one spouse sues for loss of consortium? (149)

(e) Can parents recover for the lost services, earnings and companionship of minor children? (149)

(f) What is the general rule in reference to children suing for loss of consortium? (149)

15. Under the common law what happened to a plaintiff's personal injury claim if he/she died? (149)

(a) What was the reasoning underlying this rule? (149)

(b) What happened after the passage of Lord Campbell's Act? (149)

16. What is a survival statute? (149)

(a) Do such statutes preserve a cause of action for damage to property? (149)

(b) Do they preserve personal injury claims? (149)

(c) What about claims relating to intangible interests? (150)

(d) Are these statutes applicable if the defendant (instead of the plaintiff) dies? (150)

17. What is a wrongful death statute? (150)

(a) Who brings a wrongful death claim? (150)

18. What separates the issue of wrongful death from most other areas of tort law? (150)

19. Is there a possibility of double recovery in wrongful death cases? (150)

(a) How do some states prevent double recovery? (150)

(1) Can a survival action be maintained in those states if death was instantaneous? (150)

20. Are any losses other than economic losses allowed under wrongful death legislation? Explain. (150)

21. What is the problem with wrongful death actions in which parents are seeking recovery? (150)

22. Why do spouses who have remarried want to keep that information from a jury? (150)

(a) Do most courts allow the admission of such evidence? (150)

23. Who typically brings a survival action? (151)

(a) Can creditors reach the recovery of a survival action? (151)

(b) What is one criticism of survival actions? (151)

24. What defenses do the courts generally allow to be raised in wrongful death actions? (151)

(a) What is the general rule regarding statutes of limitation in wrongful death cases? (151)

25. In what sense does a plaintiff receive a windfall by collecting for future losses in the present? (151)

(a) How does discounting awards help remedy this result? (151)

(b) How are present values calculated? (151-152)

(c) Arguably, how does inflation impact present value awards? (152)

26. What is a structured settlement? (152)

(a) What are two reasons for this kind of settlement plan? (152)

(1)

(2)

(b) What is one criticism of structured settlements? (152)

(c) Which is generally more likely to support the concept of structured settlements - the defense or plaintiff's bar? (152)

27. What is the avoidable consequences (also known as the duty to mitigate) rule? (152)

(a) How is this rule implicated in the seat belt defense? (153)

28. Can a plaintiff in a negligence case recover if she sustained no physical harm? (153)

(a) Why are damages resulting from mental suffering referred to as "parasitic" damages? (153)

(b) Why do the courts like to see some evidence of physical harm? (153)

(c) Why have the courts created an exception to this general rule in cases involving the mishandling of corpses and the negligent transmission of telegraphic messages? (153)

(d) What is the "impact rule"? (153)

(e) In what other types of cases have the courts been willing to abandon the physical harm requirement? (154)

(1)

(2)

(3)

(f) What is the "zone of danger" problem in the context of the physical harm requirement? (154)

(1) How did the <u>Dillon</u> court resolve that problem? (154)

REVIEW QUESTIONS

1. What are the different types of damages that can be awarded in a personal injury case and for what reasons are each of these awarded?

2. What problems arise in the calculation and awarding of damages?

3. What are the differences between survial actions and wrongful death actions?
   (a) What are the similarities?

4. What doctrines and rules have the courts developed to make the awarding of damages as equitable as possible?

PUTTING IT INTO PRACTICE

Your supervising attorney asks you to consider the potential problems that will have to be faced in the calculation and awarding of damages to your client, who was rendered paraplegic because of an automobile accident caused by Defendant's negligence. Your client is sixteen years old and was working at a grocery store before his injuries. He planned to become a doctor although his grades in high school made it unlikely that he would be accepted by medical schools in the United States. What problems do you anticipate you will face in helping your client recover? What arguments do you expect the defense will make?

KEY TERMS

Define the following:

Avoidable consequences rule

Collateral source rule

Derivative claim

Discounting an award

Fair market value

General damages

Loss of consortium

Parasitic damages

Present value

Special damages

Structured settlement

Survival action

Wrongful death action

The following is a certificate of compulsory arbitration. Some states require that smaller amounts (under $30,000 to $50,000) be arbitrated. Check to see if your state has compulsory arbitration.

J. Stanley Edwards
EDWARDS & EDWARDS
11000 North Scottsdale Road
Suite No. 135
Scottsdale, Arizona 85254
Tel: (602) 991-1938
Fax: (602) 991-2480
State Bar No. 004190

Attorneys for Plaintiff

IN THE SUPERIOR COURT OF THE STATE OF ARIZONA

IN AND FOR THE COUNTY OF MARICOPA

SONJA R. , Plaintiff, vs. TAMMIE D. and JOHN DOE , her husband, Defendants.	No. ____________ CERTIFICATE OF COMPULSARY ARBITRATION

The undersigned certifies that the largest award sought by the complainant, including punitive damages, but excluding interest, attorney's fees and costs does not exceed limits set by Local Rule for compulsory arbitration. This case is subject to the Uniform Rules of Procedure for Arbitration.

DATED this _____ day of April, 1992.

EDWARDS & EDWARDS

By ________________________________

J. Stanley Edwards
11000 North Scottsdale Road
Suite No. 135
Scottsdale, Arizona 85254
Attorneys for Plaintiff

In this Wrongful death suit, My client is Guardian Ad Litem For MR. T. Chicken VS. L. Weasle.

STUDY GUIDE
CHAPTER TEN

1. What is the difference between contributory negligence and comparative negligence? (163)

2. Under the doctrine of contributory negligence to whom is the burden of loss shifted? (164)

3. If a plaintiff is contributorily negligent can he/she recover if the defendant was more negligent? (164)

4. What is the rationale behind contributory negligence? (164)

(a) What is the practical explanation for the development of this doctrine in the United States? (164)

5. Why have exceptions been created to the contributory negligence rule? (164)

6. Who must plead and prove contributory negligence? (165)

7. Who decides if the plaintiff was contributorily negligent? (165)

8. What must the defendant prove in terms of causation if he/she alleges that the plaintiff was contributorily negligent? (165)

(a) What exception is made in the case of proximate cause? (165)

9. What is the last clear chance doctrine and why was it created? (165)

(a) Is this doctrine applicable if the plaintiff is helpless and the defendant does not discover the plaintiff's predicament because the defendant negligently fails to respond to it? (165)

(b) What if the plaintiff is helpless and the defendant discovers the plaintiff's situation but negligently fails to discover it because the defendant is inattentive at the time? (165)

(c) What if the plaintiff is inattentive and the defendant discovers the plaintiff's danger but negligently fails to respond to it? (166)

(d) What if neither the plaintiff nor the defendant discovers the danger because both are inattentive? (166)

(e) What if the defendant discovers the danger but cannot avoid it because of some earlier negligence on his/her part? (166-167)

(1) What name is used to describe this particular scenario? (167)

10. Is contributory negligence a defense to an intentional tort? (167)

(a) What if the defendant was "reckless" or "willful and wanton"? (167)

11. When would contributory negligence not be a defense if the defendant were negligent per se? (167)

12. What is the effect of proof of comparative negligence on a plaintiff's recovery? (168)

(a) Have most states adopted comparative negligence? (168)

13. What is the difference between a pure comparative negligence system and a 50% approach? (168)

(a) What is the difference between the "not as great as" and the "not greater than" approach? (168)

(1) When does this distinction become important? (168)

14. What problem arises in terms of assessing percentage of fault? (169)

(a) How is the problem aggravated when there are multiple defendants? (169)

15. Is the last clear chance doctrine applicable in comparative negligence jurisdictions? (169)

(a) Is comparative negligence a defense to an intentional tort? (169)

(b) Is comparative negligence a defense if the defendant is "reckless" or "willful and wanton"? (169)

(c) Is comparative negligence a defense if the defendant is negligent <u>per se</u>? (169)

16. What is the defense of assumption of risk? (169)

(a) Is a plaintiff who assumes the risk completely barred from recovery? (169-170)

17. Is there any relationship between contributory negligence and assumption of risk? If so, what is it? (170)

(a) Can a plaintiff assume the risk without being contributorily negligent? (170)

18. How have some courts distinguished between assumption of risk and contributory negligence? (170)

19. Can a defendant raise both the defense of contributory negligence and assumption of risk? (171)

(a) What is the difference between these defenses in terms of the standards used in assessing the plaintiff's conduct? (171)

(b) In what other way do these defenses differ? (171)

20. Give an example of express assumption of risk. (171)

21. Give three circumstances in which a court might not enforce an express agreement. (171)

(a)

(b)

(c)

22. What happens to the defense of assumption of risk when a state adopts a comparative negligence standard? (171)

23. Give an example of implied assumption of risk. (172)

24. Must a plaintiff actually be aware of a risk he/she impliedly assumes? (172)

(a) Must the plaintiff's consent be voluntary? (172)

(b) Is consent considered voluntary if the plaintiff has no reasonable alternative to the danger? (172)

(c) What is the result if a plaintiff resists assuming the risk but ultimately agrees to do so? (172)

(d) What is the result if a plaintiff exposes himself/herself to a risk not created by the defendant? (172)

25. Is immunity a partial or complete defense? (172)

26. Under the common law on what basis was the U.S. government granted immunity? (172)

27. For what reason was the FTCA passed? (172-173)

(a) In general what does the FTCA provide? (173)

(b) Is the U.S. government liable for intentional torts committed by federal government officials? (173)

(c) Is the federal government liable when an agency or federal employee exercises a "discretionary" function? (173)

(1) What is a "discretionary" function? (173)

28. What is the status today of sovereign immunity for the states? (174)

(a) For what reasons have many states abolished it? (174)

29. In what circumstances are local governments liable? (174)

(a) Distinguish between proprietary and governmental functions. (174)

(b) Give examples of situations in which local governments are liable. (174)

30. In what circumstances are legislators and judges immune? (174)

(a) What is the rationale for this immunity? (174)

(b) Does it matter if the public official was acting out of greed or malice? (174)

(c) Is a public official's immunity distinct from the immunity of a governmental entity? (181)

31. Under the common law could immediate family members sue one another? (182)

32. What was the rationale for spousal immunity? (182)

(a) What is the status of spousal immunity today? (182)

(b) What were the predicted consequences of the abolition of spousal immunity? (182)

(1) Have those predictions come to pass? (182)

33. What is the status of parent-child immunity today? (182)

(a) How have the courts treated the issue of negligent supervision in the context of parent-child suits? (182)

34. What is the purpose of charitable immunity? (183)

(a) What is the "trust fund" theory? (183)

(b) What is the "implied waiver" theory? (183)

(c) What is the status of charitable immunity today? (183)

35. What is the purpose of statutes of limitation? (183)

(a) When does such a statute accrue? (183)

(b) For plaintiffs what is the potential problem with these statutes? (183)

(c) What is the discovery doctrine? (183)

(1) What is one criticism of this doctrine? (184)

26. What is a statute of repose? (184)

(a) What is the purpose of such a statute? (184)

(b) When does a statute of repose begin to run? (184)

(c) What is the potential problem with such a statute? (184)

REVIEW QUESTIONS

1. Under what circumstances would you want to raise the defense of contributory/comparative negligence and when would you want to use the defense of assumption of risk?

2. What are the exceptions to the contributory negligence rule?

3. When is contributory negligence not a defense?

4. What are the possible problems that arise with the defense of comparative negligence?

5. Make a list of all the circumstances in which a defendant might be immune from suit.

PUTTING IT INTO PRACTICE

Your firm's client, Melrose Hospital, which is a non-profit institution operated by a religious organization, is being sued for negligence by a woman who received a breast implant several years ago and who is now experiencing major health problems that she attributes to this implant. What defenses might you raise on behalf of your client? Assess the likelihood of these defenses being successful.

KEY TERMS

Accrual

Assumption of risk

Comparative negligence

Contributory negligence

Discovery doctrine

Discretionary function

First clear chance case

Governmental function

Immunity

Implied waiver theory

Last clear chance doctrine

Proprietary function

Statute of limitations

Statute of repose

Trust fund theory

The following pages contain a copy of a police report.

Affirmative Defense

Motion For Summary Judgement

M

1989 JUN 15 PM 4:59

ARIZONA TRAFFIC ACCIDENT REPORT

FORWARD COPY TO ARIZONA DEPARTMENT OF TRANSPORTATION ACCIDENT RECORDS ANALYSIS UNIT 222E 205 S. 17th AVE., PHOENIX, ARIZONA 85007

1

INJURY SEVERITY CLASSIFICATION: 1 NO INJURY; 2 POSSIBLE INJURY; 3 NON-INCAPACITATING EVIDENT; 4 INCAPACITATING; 5 FATAL; 6 UNKNOWN

REPORT ID — DATE: YEAR 89 MONTH DAY — HOUR 1330

NCIC NO. — OFFICER'S ID NO. 00222 — DAY OF WK

AGENCY USE — AGENCY REPORT NUMBER: Scottsdale Police Dept. 89-

TOTAL NO. OF SHEETS 3

2 TOTAL UNITS 2 — TOTAL INJURIES 0 — TOTAL FATALITIES 0 — ESTIMATED TOTAL DAMAGE: ☒ OVER MINIMUM ☐ UNDER MINIMUM — ☐ FATAL ☐ HIT/RUN ☐ GOVT. PROP. — DISTRICT OR GRID NO. 010015

3 LOCATION — NAME OF STREET OR HIGHWAY ON Civic Center Blvd. — ☒ INSIDE ☐ OUTSIDE — CITY Scottsdale — COUNTY Maricopa

INTERSECTING STREET, ROAD /M.P. OR R.P. ☒ AT ☐ FROM 1st Ave — ☐ NORTH ☐ EAST ☐ SOUTH ☐ WEST — ☐ PLUS ☐ MINUS — DISTANCE — ☐ MILES ☐ FEET

4

TRAFFIC UNIT NO. 1

STATE Az — CLASS 2 — LICENSE OR SOCIAL SECURITY NUMBER — ☒ DRIVER ☐ PEDESTRIAN ☐ PEDALCYCLIST — NAME — SEX M — INJ 1

RESTRICTIONS — DATE OF BIRTH 020710 — ADDRESS Via de Belleza — CITY Scottsdale, Az — STATE

PLATE NUMBER — STATE Az — YEAR 2/90 — ☒ SAME AS DRIVER — OWNER'S NAME — ADDRESS — CITY — STATE

COLOR Beige — YEAR 80 — MAKE Cadillac — BODY STYLE 4 Dr. — ☐ CAMPER — VIN — RESTRAINT USED ☐ YES ☒ NO ☐ UNK

REMOVED TO Service — REMOVED BY Service — ORDERS OF Police — POSTED SPEED LIMIT 30 — OFC EST SPEED 10 — OFC EST REAS 0

TRAILER (OTHER UNIT) PLATE NO — STATE — YEAR — DESCRIPTION OF TRAILER OR OTHER UNIT — DR'S EST SPEED 10±

TRAFFIC UNIT NO. 2

STATE Az — CLASS 2 — LICENSE OR SOCIAL SECURITY NO. — ☒ DRIVER ☐ PEDESTRIAN ☐ PEDALCYCLIST — NAME — SEX M — INJ 1

RESTRICTIONS — DATE OF BIRTH 063064 — ADDRESS Beverly Ln. — CITY Phx. Az — STATE

PLATE NUMBER — STATE Az — YEAR 7/89 — ☐ SAME AS DRIVER — OWNER'S NAME — ADDRESS N. 40th St. #215 — CITY Phx. — STATE Az

COLOR Maroon — YEAR 85 — MAKE Mazda — BODY STYLE 2 Door — ☐ CAMPER — VIN — RESTRAINT USED ☐ YES ☒ NO ☐ UNK

REMOVED TO Service — REMOVED BY Driver — ORDERS OF Police — POSTED SPEED LIMIT 30 — OFC EST SPEED — OFC EST REAS

TRAILER (OTHER UNIT) PLATE NO. — STATE — YEAR — DESCRIPTION OF TRAILER OR OTHER UNIT — DR'S EST SPEED 35

5 PASSENGERS

SEATING POSITION DIAGRAM: 07 04 01 / 08 05 02 / 09 06 03 — 10 NOT IN PASSENGER COMPART. 11 MOTORCYCLE, BUS. 12 OTHER 13 UNKNOWN 14 PEDALCYCLE

RU- RESTRAINT USED: Y-YES N-NO UN-UNK — HU- HELMET USAGE: Y-YES N-NO UK-UNK

INJURED TAKEN TO/BY: N/A

UNIT	SEAT POS	RU	NAME	ADDRESS	CITY	STATE	HU	AGE	SEX	INJ

6 OTHER PROPERTY DAMAGE (DESCRIBE)

OWNER'S NAME — ADDRESS — CITY — STATE — TELEPHONE NUMBER

7 WITNESSES

NAME	ADDRESS	CITY	STATE	TELEPHONE NUMBER	AGE
		Phx Az			40±

8 ARRESTS

03

NAME	A.R.S. NO. OR CITY CODE	CITATION/ARREST NUMBER(S)
	28-774	
	28-1253-D; 28-701.A	

9 PHOTOS TAKEN ☐ YES ☒ NO — PHOTOGRAPHER'S NAME, ID NUMBER, AND AGENCY — INVEST AT SCENE ☒ YES ☐ NO — DATE INVEST. 061489 — TIME INVEST 1340

OFFICER'S SIGNATURE AND ID NUMBER — AGENCY Scottsdale Police Dept. — DATE COMPLETED 061489

89.10[redacted]

10 - DIAGRAM

Doubletree Inn

Doubletree Inn

35'

35'

82'

1st Ave

Civic Center Blvd

11 - INDICATE NORTH

12 - SKIDDING OCCURED — INDICATE WHICH VEHICLES SKIDDED BY NUMBER

X YES _ NO — veh. 2

13 - ACCIDENT MEASUREMENTS

P.I.

22' w/E Civ. Ctr. Blvd

1' s/s 1st Ave.

(87' skid - veh. 2)

15 - CLASSIFICATION BY TYPE

YES NO
_ X RAN OFF ROADWAY PRIOR TO FIRST HARMFUL EVENT

COLLISION BETWEEN A MOTOR VEHICLE IN TRANSPORT AND
1 _ PEDESTRIAN
2 X MOTOR VEHICLE
3 _ RAILWAY TRAIN
4 _ PEDALCYCLIST
5 _ ANIMAL
6 _ FIXED OBJECT
7 _ OTHER OBJECT

NONCOLLISION INVOLVING A MOTOR VEHICLE IN TRANSPORT
8 _ OVERTURNING
9 _ OTHER NONCOLLISION

14 - DESCRIBE WHAT HAPPENED

Veh. 1 exiting private drive to cross Civic Center Blvd was struck by veh. 2, N/B on Civic Center Blvd.

16 - LIGHT CONDITION
CHECK ONLY ONE
1 X DAYLIGHT
2 _ DAWN OR DUSK
3 _ DARKNESS

YES NO
1 X _ STREET LIGHT
2 _ X STREET LIGHT FUNCTIONING

17 - WEATHER CONDITIONS
CHECK ONLY ONE
1 X CLEAR
2 _ RAINING
3 _ CLOUDY
4 _ SNOWING
5 _ STRONG WIND
6 _ DUST
7 _ FOG

18 - ROAD SURFACE TYPE
CHECK ONLY ONE
1 X ASPHALT
2 _ CONCRETE
3 _ GRAVEL
4 _ DIRT
5 _ OTHER

19 - TYPE OF LOCATION
CHECK ONLY ONE
1 X INTERSECTION
2 _ JUNCTION AREA
3 _ NON-JUNCTION AREA
4 _ DRIVEWAY ACCESS
5 _ ALLEY ACCESS

20 - INTERSECTION RELATED
X YES _ NO

21 - SPECIAL LOCATION
CHECK ONLY ONE
1 _ SCHOOL CROSSING
2 _ PEDESTRIAN CROSSWALK (STRIPED)
3 _ PEDESTRIAN CROSSWALK (NO STRIPING)
4 _ BRIDGE
5 _ TUNNEL
6 _ RR CROSSING
7 _ ALLEY
8 _ BIKE PATH
9 _ 2-WAY LEFT TURN LANE

22 - UNUSUAL ROAD CONDITION
CHECK ONLY ONE
1 _ UNDER CONSTRUCTION, TRAFFIC ALLOWED
2 _ UNDER CONSTRUCTION NO TRAFFIC ALLOWED
3 _ UNDER REPAIRS
4 _ HOLES, RUTS, BUMPS
5 _ OBSTRUCTION - PROTECTED
6 _ OBSTRUCTION - UNPROTECTED
7 _ OBSTRUCTION - UNLIGHTED AT NIGHT
8 _ DEFECTIVE SHOULDERS
9 _ CHANGING ROAD WIDTH
10 _ FLOODED
11 _ TEMPORARY LANE CLOSURE

23 - TRAFFIC CONTROL DEVICES
LEGEND A - DEVICE PRESENT
B - DAMAGED OR NON-FUNCTIONAL PRIOR TO ACCIDENT

CHECK ANY THAT APPLY
A B
1 _ _ STOP AND GO SIGNAL
2 _ _ YIELD SIGN
3 X _ STOP SIGN
4 _ _ WARNING SIGN
5 _ _ RAILROAD SIGNAL
6 _ _ FLASHING SIGNAL
7 _ _ FLAGMAN OR OFFICER

24 - NON-INTERSECTION ROAD CHARACTER
CHECK ONLY ONE
1 _ 2-WAY STRIPED CENTERLINE
2 _ 2-WAY, NO STRIPE
3 _ 2-WAY, PAINTED MEDIAN
4 X 2-WAY, RAISED MEDIAN
5 _ 2-WAY, BARRIER MEDIAN
6 _ 2-WAY, DEPRESSED MEDIAN
7 _ 2-WAY, EXTENDED MEDIAN
8 _ 1-WAY STREET

25 - ROAD GRADE
CHECK ONLY ONE
1 _ LEVEL
2 _ DOWNGRADE
3 X UPGRADE
4 _ HILLCREST
5 _ DIP

26 - UNUSUAL ROAD SURFACE CONDITION
CHECK ONLY ONE
1 _ WET
2 _ LOOSE SAND, DIRT OR GRAVEL
3 _ SNOWY, ICY
4 _ FRESH OIL
5 _ OTHER
6 _ UNKNOWN

27 - PHYSICAL CONDITION
TWO CHOICES PER PERSON MAY BE SELECTED
1 2
1 X X NO APPARENT DEFECTS
2 _ _ HAD BEEN DRINKING
3 _ _ APPEARED TO BE UNDER INFLUENCE OF DRUGS
4 _ _ ILL - ABILITY INFLUENCED
5 _ _ SLEEPY - FATIGUED
6 _ _ OTHER BODILY DEFECTS, INFIRMITIES
7 _ _ UNKNOWN

28 - VIOLATIONS BEHAVIOR
TWO CHOICES PER PERSON MAY BE SELECTED
1 2
1 _ _ NO IMPROPER DRIVING
2 _ X SPEED TOO FAST FOR CONDITIONS
3 _ _ EXCEEDED LAWFUL SPEED
4 X _ FAILED TO YIELD RIGHT-OF-WAY
5 _ _ FOLLOWED TOO CLOSELY
6 _ _ RAN STOP SIGN
7 _ _ DISREGARDED TRAFFIC SIGNAL
8 _ _ MADE IMPROPER TURN
9 _ _ DROVE IN OPPOSING TRAFFIC LANE
10 _ _ KNOWINGLY OPERATED WITH FAULTY OR MISSING EQUIPMENT
11 _ _ REQUIRED MOTORCYCLE SAFETY EQUIPMENT NOT USED
12 _ _ PASSED IN NO PASSING ZONE
13 _ _ UNSAFE LANE CHANGE
14 _ _ OTHER UNSAFE PASSING
15 _ _ INATTENTION
16 _ _ DID NOT USE CROSSWALK
17 _ _ WALKED ON WRONG SIDE OF ROAD
18 _ _ OTHER
19 _ _ UNKNOWN

29 - VEHICLE CONDITION
TWO CHOICES PER VEHICLE MAY BE SELECTED
1 2
1 X X NO APPARENT DEFECTS
2 _ _ DEFECTIVE BRAKES
3 _ _ DEFECTIVE STEERING
4 _ _ DEFECTIVE HEADLIGHTS
5 _ _ DEFECTIVE TAIL LIGHTS
6 _ _ DEFECTIVE TURN-SIGNAL
7 _ _ PUNCTURE OR BLOWOUT
8 _ _ ONE OR MORE SMOOTH TIRES
9 _ _ FIRE
10 _ _ DEFECTIVE WINDSHIELD WIPER
11 _ _ DEFECTIVE EXHAUST SYSTEM
12 _ _ OTHER DEFECTS
13 _ _ NO TRAILER BRAKES
14 _ _ UNKNOWN

30 - TRAFFIC UNIT ACTION
CHECK ONE PER UNIT
1 2
1 _ X GOING STRAIGHT AHEAD
2 _ _ SLOWING IN TRAFFICWAY
3 _ _ STOPPED IN TRAFFICWAY
4 _ _ MAKING LEFT TURN
5 _ _ MAKING RIGHT TURN
6 _ _ MAKING U TURN
7 _ _ ENTERING ALLEY OR DRIVEWAY
8 X _ LEAVING ALLEY OR DRIVEWAY
9 _ _ OVERTAKING/PASSING
10 _ _ CHANGING LANES
11 _ _ BACKING
12 _ _ AVOIDING VEHICLE, OBJECT, PEDESTRIAN
13 _ _ ENTERING PARKING POSITION
14 _ _ LEAVING PARKING POSITION
15 _ _ PROPERLY PARKED
16 _ _ IMPROPERLY PARKED
17 _ _ DRIVERLESS MOVING VEHICLE
18 _ _ CROSSING ROAD
19 _ _ WALKING WITH TRAFFIC
20 _ _ WALKING AGAINST TRAFFIC
21 _ _ STANDING
22 _ _ LYING
23 _ _ GETTING ON OR OFF VEHICLE
24 _ _ WORKING ON OR PUSHING VEHICLE
25 _ _ WORKING ON ROAD
26 _ _ OTHER
27 _ _ UNKNOWN

31 - VISION OBSCUREMENT
CHECK ONE PER UNIT
1 2
1 X X NOT OBSCURED
2 _ _ BY PARKED STOPPED VEHICLE
3 _ _ BY MOVING VEHICLE
4 _ _ BY BUILDING
5 _ _ BY EMBANKMENT
6 _ _ BY SIGNBOARD
7 _ _ BY HILLCREST
8 _ _ BY LOAD ON VEHICLE
9 _ _ BY TREES, BUSHES
10 _ _ BY HEADLIGHT
11 _ _ BY SUN GLARE
12 _ _ BECAUSE OF BAD WEATHER
13 _ _ OTHER
14 _ _ RAIN, SNOW, FOG ON WINDSHIELD
15 _ _ WINDSHIELD OBSCURED - OTHER
16 _ _ UNKNOWN

32 - MOTORCYCLE HELMET USED
CHECK ONE PER UNIT
1 2
_ _ YES
_ _ NO
_ _ UNKNOWN

ACCIDENT WITNESS STATEMENT

Police Department Scottsdale Arizona

DR # ____________

Reporting Officer ____________ No. ____

DATE 6/14 TIME 1:30 pm LOCATION OF ACCIDENT 1st AVE & CIVIC CENTER

COMPLETE ONLY THOSE SPACES THAT APPLY TO YOU

DRIVER (X) PASSENGER ( ) WITNESS ( )

PLEASE PRINT

LAST NAME	FIRST NAME	MIDDLE NAME
—	PAUL	DAVID

CURRENT MAILING ADDRESS. (include City, State and Zip Code)
E BEVERLY LN. PHX AZ. 85032

BUSINESS NAME/ADDRESS: (include City, State and Zip Code)
MARKETING CORPORATION

HOME TELEPHONE:

BUSINESS TELEPHONE: —

DATE OF BIRTH: 6-30-64

DRIVERS LICENSE NUMBER:

DRIVER ONLY: INSURANCE COMPANY
INSURANCE HOTLINE

POLICY NUMBER:

WHAT WERE YOU DOING JUST PRIOR TO THE ACCIDENT OCCURRING?
HEADING NORTH ON CIVIC CENTER, APPROACHING STOP ~~SIGN~~, LIGHT.

WHAT CALLED YOUR ATTENTION TO THE ACCIDENT? (breaking glass, etc.)
OTHER VEHICLE INVOLVED RAN STOP SIGN AND CUT RIGHT IN FRONT OF ME. I HIT MY BRAKES BUT ~~[illegible]~~ COULD NOT AVOID HIM.

HOW FAR AWAY FROM THE ACCIDENT WERE YOU WHEN IT OCCURRED?

WHAT WAS YOUR SPEED? 35 mph WHAT WAS YOUR DIRECTION OF TRAVEL? NORTH

HOW MANY VEHICLES WERE INVOLVED IN THE ACCIDENT? 2

IDENTIFY THE VEHICLES INVOLVED (example: red Ford station wagon)

	color	make	body style
Vehicle No. 1	RED	MAZDA	HATCHBACK GLC DELUX
Vehicle No. 2	BEIGE	CADILAC	FLEETWOOD BROUGHAM
Vehicle No. 3			

WEATHER CONDITIONS: (check only those that applied at accident time)

(X) clear ( ) raining ( ) cloudy ( ) strong wind ( ) dust ( ) fog

THIS SECTION TO BE COMPLETED ONLY BY DRIVERS AND PASSENGERS OF VEHICLES INVOLVED IN THE ACCIDENT

LIST ALL PASSENGERS HERE (please print)

Name	Address	City	State	Zip	Phone	Age	Sex
PAUL							

Form 195.0 (Rev. 12/84) PD 02881 (8/84)

POLICE DEPARTMENT SCOTTSDALE ARIZONA
ACCIDENT WITNESS STATEMENT

DESCRIPTION OF ACCIDENT:

____

____

____

____

____

____

____

____

____

YOUR SIGNATURE HERE	WITNESSED BY (OFFICER)

INSTRUCTIONS

(1) INDICATE **NORTH** BY PLACING AN ARROW POINTING NORTH IN THE BOX PROVIDED BELOW.
(2) USING THE LINED AREA BELOW, DRAW A DIAGRAM WHICH SHOWS THE LOCATION OF THE VEHICLES AT THE TIME THE ACCIDENT OCCURRED.
(3) USE A SOLID LINE TO SHOW THE PATH OF THE VEHICLES **BEFORE** THE ACCIDENT OCCURRED.
(4) NUMBER EACH VEHICLE ACCORDING TO THE NUMBERS YOU USED ON THE OTHER SIDE OF THIS PAGE.

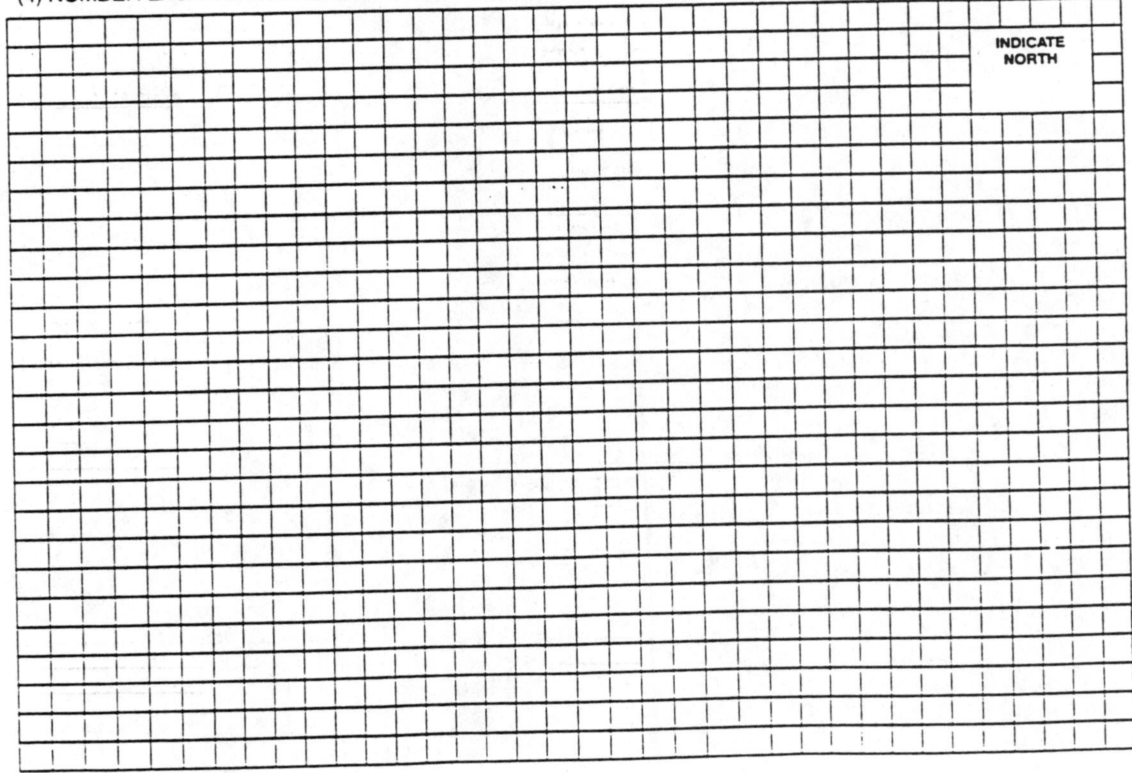

STUDY GUIDE
CHAPTER ELEVEN

1. Why is defamation considered one of the most complex torts? (191-192)

2. What is the difference between libel and slander? (182)

(a) Is the distinction between the two always clear? (192)

3. Define "special harm." (192)

(a) When must special harm be proved? (192)

4. What are the four exceptions to the special harm requirement for slander? (192)

(a)

(b)

(c)

(d)

5. What are presumed damages? (192)

(a) Why is it advantageous to a plaintiff when damages are presumed? (192-193)

(b) In cases involving matters of public concern what must a plaintiff prove before he/she can be awarded presumed damages? (193)

6. What must a plaintiff who is alleging defamation prove? (193)

(a)

(b)

(c)

7. Must the plaintiff's reputation actually be harmed? (193)

(a) Must everyone who hears the defamatory statement believe it to be true? .(193)

(b) Must the plaintiff's reputation be soiled in the eyes of the whole community? (194)

(c) Must the plaintiff show that the defendant referred to him by name? (194)

(d) Can the plaintiff recover if the defendant makes a defamatory statement in reference to a group of which the plaintiff is a member? (194)

8. Must a statement be subject to only a defamatory interpretation if the plaintiff is to recover? (194)

9. What is "innuendo"? (194)

(a) Give an example of a situation in which a plaintiff would be required to show the innuendo in a complaint. (194)

10. Can a plaintiff recover if a defendant's statement is substantially true? (195)

11. Who has the burden of proving that a statement is true or false? (195)

12. Can someone who is deceased be defamed? (195)

(a) Can a corporation, partnership or association be defamed? (195)

13. Can a statement that is clearly an opinion be defamatory? (195)

(a) What if the statement implies factual matters? (195)

14. What does a court look at in determining whether a statement is fact or opinion? (195)

(a)

(b)

(c)

(d)

15. What is meant by the term "publication" in terms of defamation? (195)

(a) Must publication be intentional? (196)

(b) Is a statement published if it is simply overheard by someone? (196)

(c) Must the person who hears the statement understand it? (196)

(d) Is repetition considered publication? (196)

(e) Must the person repeating the statement believe it to be true? (196)

(f) What is the single publication rule? (196)

16. What was the holding in <u>New York Times v. Sullivan</u>? (196)

(a) How did the Court define "actual malice"? (196)

(b) What types of plaintiffs must prove actual malice? (196)

17. How does one become a public figure? (196)

18. Why does the Court give less protection to public figures and public officials than other types of plaintiffs? (196)

19. Can a defendant ever be held strictly liable for a defamatory statement? (197)

20. What can a successful plaintiff recover in a defamation case? (204)

(a) Can punitive damages be awarded? (204)

(b) When can presumed damages be awarded? (204)

(c) Why might a plaintiff be willing to accept nominal damages? (204)

21. What is a retraction statute? (205)

22. What is the difference between an absolute and qualified privilege? (205)

23. What types of people enjoy absolute immunity for statements made during the course and furtherance of their duties? (205)

(a)

(b)

(c)

(d)

24. Are husband-wife communications absolutely privileged? (206)

25. In what types of situations do people enjoy a qualified privilege? (206)

(a)

(b)

(c)

26. Is making a statement for the purposes of gaining a competitive advantage privileged? (206)

27. Is a defendant qualifiedly privileged if he is acting for the protection of the recipient of the information? (206)

28. Can a qualified privilege be lost if it is abused? (206)

REVIEW QUESTIONS

1. Why is it important to distinguish between libel and slander?

2. What must a plaintiff who is alleging defamation prove? Anticipate the potential problems that may arise with respect to each element of defamation.

3. In what respects is it easier for a private individual to recover for defamation than for a public figure?

4. Under what circumstances can an individual claim privilege as a response to a defamation claim?

PUTTING IT INTO PRACTICE

A public school teacher wants to sue the assistant principal for defamation. She claims that the principal prepared an evaluation after a classroom visitation and that the evaluation falsely represented what had occurred during his visit. As a result of this evaluation the assistant principal recommended to the principal that the teacher be terminated. This recommendation was conveyed to the school board and she was terminated. She claims that the assistant principal also spoke to several of her peers about what he had observed in her classroom and she maintains that what he represented to them was erroneous.

Explain what she must prove if she is to bring a successful defamation claim. Advise her of the potential pitfalls if she were to attempt to bring suit.

KEY TERMS

Define the following:

Absolute privilege

Actual malice

Defamation

Innuendo

Libel

Pecuniary

Publication

Public figure

Presumed damages

Qualified privilege

Retraction statute

Single publication rule

Slander

Slander _per se_

Special harm

The following pages contain a sample summons.

De Murrer

De-Shouter

J. Stanley Edwards
EDWARDS & EDWARDS
11000 North Scottsdale Road
Suite No. 135
Scottsdale, Arizona 85254
Tel: (602) 991-1938
Fax: (602) 991-2480
State Bar No. 004190

Attorneys for Plaintiff

IN THE SUPERIOR COURT OF THE STATE OF ARIZONA

IN AND FOR THE COUNTY OF MARICOPA

SONJA R. Plaintiff, vs. TAMMIE D. and JOHN DOE , her husband, Defendants.	No. ______________ SUMMONS

THE STATE OF ARIZONA TO THE DEFENDANTS:

TAMMIE D. and JOHN DOE her husband

YOU ARE HEREBY SUMMONED and required to appear and defend, within the time applicable, in this action in this Court. If served within Arizona, you shall appear and defend within **TWENTY** days after the service of the Summons and Complaint upon you, exclusive of the day of service. If served out of the State of Arizona - whether by direct service, by registered or certified mail, or by publication - you shall appear and defend within **THIRTY** days after the service of the Summons and Complaint upon you is complete, exclusive of the day of service. Where process is served upon the Arizona Director of Insurance as an insurer's attorney to receive service of legal process against it in this State, the insurer shall not be required to appear, answer or plead until expiration of **FORTY** days after date of such service upon the Director. Service by registered or certified mail without the State of Arizona is complete **THIRTY** days after the date of filing the receipt and Affidavit of Service with the Court. Service by publication is complete **THIRTY** days after the date of first publication. Direct service is complete when made. Service upon the Arizona Motor Vehicle Superintendent is complete **THIRTY** days after filing the Affidavit of Compliance and return receipt or Officer's Return. **RCP 4; ARS 20-222, 28-502, 28-503.**

YOU ARE HEREBY NOTIFIED that in case of your failure to appear and defend within the time applicable, Judgment by default may be rendered against you for the relief demanded in the Complaint.

YOU ARE CAUTIONED that in order to appear and defend, you must file an Answer or proper response in writing with the Clerk of this Court, accompanied by the necessary filing fee, within the time required, and you are required to serve a copy of any Answer or response upon the Plaintiffs' attorney. **RCP 10(d); ARS 12-311; RCP 5.**

The name and address of the attorneys for Plaintiffs is: J. Stanley Edwards, EDWARDS & EDWARDS, 11000 North Scottsdale Road, Suite No. 135, Scottsdale, Arizona 85254.

SIGNED AND SEALED this Date:

____

JUDITH ALLEN, CLERK

By ____________________________
Deputy Clerk

J. Stanley Edwards
EDWARDS & EDWARDS
11000 North Scottsdale Road
Suite No. 135
Scottsdale, Arizona 85254
(602) 991-1938

STUDY GUIDE
CHAPTER TWELVE

1. What is required of a professional in terms of duty of care? (213)

2. Explain the dilemma surrounding the use of a national or local standard when determining standard of care. (213)

3. Does an unfavorable outcome necessarily mean a professional was negligent? (213)

4. What is the standard of care expected of an attorney as described in Procanik v. Cillo? (220-222)

5. If other professionals testify that they would have used a procedure different from that used by the defendant professional, is the defendant necessarily negligent? Explain. (223)

(a) Do you think professionals who use unorthodox procedures are more likely to be found negligent than their more conventional counterparts? (223-224)

6. What are the possible things that a professional could do that could be deemed neligent? (223-224)

(a)

(b)

(c)

(d)

(e)

7. To what standard of care are specialists held? (224)

(a) How does that standard of care compare to the standard of care for generalists? (224)

(b) Must specialists adhere to a local or national standard? (224)

(1) Why? (224)

8. What is a fiduciary relationship and how does it relate to the informed consent doctrine? (224-225)

(a) Why is this doctrine particularly important in the medical field? (225)

9. In accordance with the informed consent doctrine what is a physician obligated to tell a patient? (225)

(a) What factors increase a physician's duty to warn? (225)

(b) Is a physician obligated to tell a patient about alternative treatments? (225)

(c) Does a physician have an obligation to inform a patient in an emergency situation? (225)

(d) Do the courts look at the expectations of patients or the practices within the medical community in deciding what should and should not be disclosed to patients? (225)

(e) For what reason might a physician opt not to disclose a risk to a patient? (225)

(1) When is a risk considered material and therefore one that a physician is obligated to disclose? (225)

10. In what types of cases might a plaintiff opt to sue on the basis of battery? (226)

(a) What are the practical differences between a battery and a negligence claim? (226)

11. What kind of expert testimony is necessary in a malpractice case? (226)

(a) How does the locality rule affect the testimony that must be provided? (226)

12. What must a defendant professional prove if he/she alleges contributory negligence? (226-227)

13. Under what circumstances might a defendant rely on the defense of assumption of risk? (227)

14. What is the defense of emergency? (227)

(a) What must the defendant prove if he/she alleges an emergency existed? (227)

15. Why is it important for a professional to maintain adequate records? (228)

16. Can a patient usually gain access to his/her medical records? (228)

(a) Can a defendant usually gain access to a plaintiff's medical records via a subpoena? (228)

17. Are professional negligence claims on the increase? (228)

18. What are some of the reasons behind many malpractice claims? (228-229)

(a)

(b)

19. What can professionals do to improve client relations? (229)

(a)

(b)

(c)

20. What might legal assistants do to improve client relations? (229-230)

(a)

(b)

21. Why is it important to consult the statutes when you become involved in litigating a malpractice claim? (230)

REVIEW QUESTIONS

1. How is the standard of care to which professionals are held defined?

2. What are the most likely reasons that a professional will have a professional negligence claim filed against him/her? What might professionals do to avoid such claims?

3. What can a professional argue in response to a professional negligence claim?

4. What types of information are professionals obligated to disclose to their clients? Why is disclosure particularly important and also problematic in the medical arena?

PUTTING IT INTO PRACTICE

You take your dog to the vet to have the dog's teeth cleaned. When you bring your dog home he appears very lethargic, which your vet assures you is normal after this procedure. Your dog's condition, however, worsens and he ultimately dies. What will you have to prove if you want to bring a professional negligence claim against your vet? What will your vet likely argue in response?

KEY TERMS

Define the following:

Fiduciary relationship

Informed consent

Locality rule

National standard

The following is a sample list of witnesses and exhibits.

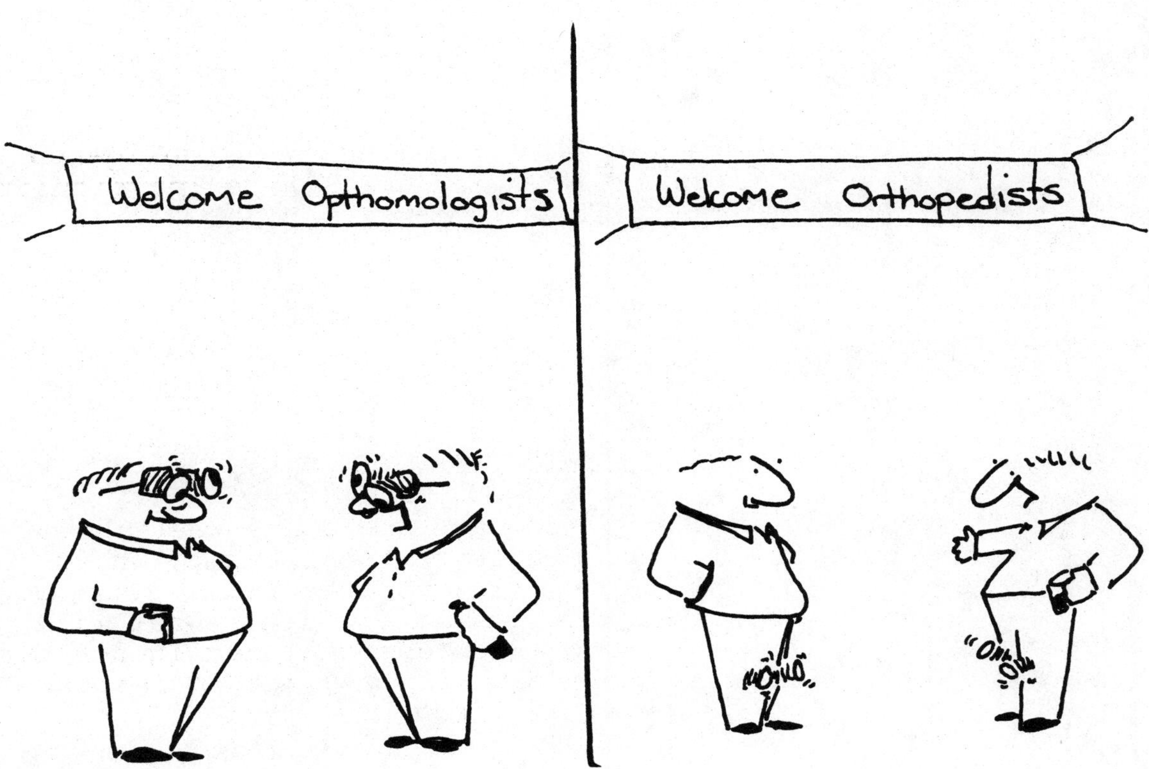

J. Stanley Edwards
EDWARDS & EDWARDS
10505 North 69th Street
Suite No. 800
Scottsdale, Arizona 85253
(602) 991-1938
State Bar No. 004190

Attorneys for Plaintiff

Edwards & Edwards
Attorneys at Law
10505 North 69th Street, Suite 800 • Scottsdale, Arizona 85253 • (602) 991-1938

IN THE SUPERIOR COURT OF THE STATE OF ARIZONA

IN AND FOR THE COUNTY OF MARICOPA

MARC A. , a single man, Plaintiff, vs. BERNADETTE , et vir., Defendants.	No. CV PLAINTIFF'S LIST OF WITNESSES AND EXHIBITS (Assigned to the Hon. Jonathan Schwartz)

Plaintiff, by and through counsel undersigned, pursuant to the Rules of Uniform Practice, rule V(a), hereby files his List of Witnesses and Exhibits as follows:

WITNESSES

1. Marc A.
2. Leon "Skip"
3. Joanne ,
4. Jodean ;
5. Dr. Anthony T. M. D.;
6. Dr. Lynne , D. O.;
7. Dr. Brad L. M. D.;

8. Dr. Albert , D. C.

9. Representative of Eagle Medical Services, Inc.;

10. Representative of Humana Hospital Desert Valley;

11. Representative of Scottsdale Memorial Hospital - North;

12. Any and all witnesses listed by Defendants.

EXHIBITS

1. Medical records, billing statements and reports of Dr. Anthony T. , M. D.;

2. Medical records, billing statements and reports of Dr. Lynne D. O.;

3. Medical records, billing statements and reports of Dr. Brad L. M. D.;

4. Medical records, billing statements and reports of Dr. Albert D. C.;

5. Medical records of Eagle Medical Services, Inc.;

6. Medical records of Humana Hospital Desert Valley;

7. Medical records of Scottsdale Memorial Hospital - North;

9. Deposition of Plaintiff taken August 27, 1991;

10. Any depositions to be taken in the future relating to this case;

11. Any and all Uniform and Non-Uniform Interrogatories and Answers thereto propounded by any party in this case;

12. Any and all Requests for Production of Documents and Responses thereto of any party relating to this case.

13. Any and all Requests for Admission and Answers thereto of

Edwards & Edwards
Attorneys at Law
10505 North 69th Street, Suite 800 • Scottsdale, Arizona 85253 • (602) 991-1938

any party relating to this case.

14. Any and all exhibits listed by Defendants.

Plaintiff reserves the right to amend and/or supplement his List of Witnesses and Exhibits at any time prior to trial of this matter.

DATED this 13 day of September, 1991.

EDWARDS & EDWARDS

By ____________________
J. Stanley Edwards
10505 North 69th Street
Suite No. 800
Scottsdale, Arizona 85253
Attorneys for Plaintiff

COPY of the foregoing
mailed/delivered this
13 day of September,
1991, to:

Suite No. 230
Phoenix, Arizona 85014
Attorneys for Defendants

ORIGINAL of the foregoing
delivered this 13 day
of September, 1991, to:

Clerk of the Superior Court
Central Courts Building
201 West Jefferson Street
Phoenix, Arizona 85003

____
J. Stanley Edwards

STUDY GUIDE
CHAPTER THIRTEEN

1. What are three areas where strict liability is applicable? (236)

(a)

(b)

(c)

2. Why is the term "absolute liability" somewhat misleading? (236)

(a) Is the term "liability without fault synonymous with the term "strict liability"? (236)

3. What is the distinction between negligence and strict liability? (236)

4. What is the majority rule regarding trespassing animals? (237)

(a) How does the majority rule compare with the English common law? (237)

(b) What is a "fencing in" statute? (237)

(c) What is a "fencing out" statute? (237)

5. What is the rule regarding wild animals? (237)

(a) Are domesticated animals considered dangerous? (237)

(b) When is strict liability imposed in reference to domesticated animals? (237)

(c) Does the "one free bite" rule protect dog owners from liability? (237)

6. What rule evolved from Rylands? (238)

7. What are the elements of an "abnormally dangerous" activity according to the Restatement? (238)

(a) Must all these factors be present to have strict liability? (238)

(b) What is the essential question when dealing with an "abnormally dangerous" activity? (238)

(c) Can you automatically categorize any activity as "abnormally dangerous" or must you consider the specific facts surrounding the activity? (238)

8. Give an example of an "abnormally dangerous" activity and explain why it is classified as such. (244)

9. Why is the flying of airplanes not considered "abnormally dangerous" today? (245)

10. Give an example of an activity that is not considered "abnormally dangerous" and explain why it is classified as such. (245)

11. In what way does public policy influence the courts' classification of activities as either "abnormally dangerous" or not? (245)

12. What are two reasons underlying strict liability in the product liability area? (246)

(a)

(b)

13. What are two limitations on strict liability? (246)

(a)

(b)

14. In what situations will a court find lack of proximate cause in a strict liability case? (246)

(a)

(b)

(c)

15. Why is it that a pedestrian run over by a truck transporting dynamite cannot sue on the basis of strict liability? (246)

16. Use Foster v. Preston Mills to illustrate the idea of an "abnormally sensitive" activity. (246)

(a) What rule of law came out of that case? (246)

17. What is the rule regarding "acts of God"? (246-247)

18. Are courts more or less likely to find proximate cause in strict liabliity cases than they are in negligence cases? (247)

(a) Explain your answer. (247)

19. Are courts more or less likely to find liability when there is an unforeseen, intervening cause in a strict liability case than in a negligence case? (247)

(a) Explain your answer. (247)

20. Give an example of a situation in which a defendant may be able to argue assumption of risk in a strict liability case. (247)

21. Is contributory negligence a defense to strict liability? (247)

REVIEW QUESTIONS

1. In what situations might a person be held strictly liable?

2. What factors are taken into consideration when deciding whether one should be strictly liable for his/her conduct?

3. What defenses might one raise in response to a strict liability claim?

PUTTING IT INTO PRACTICE

A farmer sets a carefully controlled bonfire on his property. Unfortunately, a sudden and powerful wind comes up and ignites some grass in the vicinity and the fire immediately spreads to a neighboring forest, resulting in the destruction of hundreds of acres of state-owned forestland. Assuming the farmer is not negligent in setting the fire, what would the state have to argue if it wanted to find the farmer strictly liable for the property damage? What might the farmer argue in his defense?

KEY TERMS

Define the following:

Abnormally dangerous activity

Absolute liability

Fencing in statutes

Fencing out statutes

Strict liability

The following pages contain a sample of a request for production of documents and things.

J. Stanley Edwards
EDWARDS & EDWARDS
10505 North 69th Street
Suite No. 800
Scottsdale, Arizona 85253
(602) 991-1938
State Bar No. 004190

Attorneys for Plaintiff

IN THE SUPERIOR COURT OF THE STATE OF ARIZONA

IN AND FOR THE COUNTY OF MARICOPA

PAUL D. , a single man, Plaintiff, vs. GEORGE B. PECK and EDITH PECK, husband and wife, Defendants.	No. CV 91- REQUEST FOR PRODUCTION OF DOCUMENTS TO DEFENDANTS

This party requests that the documents or things designated in the attached Exhibit "A" be produced for inspection and copying. **RCP 34.**

Except as provided otherwise in the attached Exhibit "A", the time and place of inspection are:

TIME: 10:00 A. M., December 19, 1991

PLACE: J. Stanley Edwards, Edwards & Edwards, 10505 North 69th Street, Suite No. 800, Scottsdale, Arizona 85253

The attached Exhibit "A" sets forth the items to be inspected, either by individual item or by category; describes each item and category with reasonable particularity; and specifies the reasonable time, place and manner of making the inspection and performing the related acts in connection with each item.

The party upon whom this Request is served shall serve a written response with **THIRTY (30)** days after the service of the Request, except that a Defendant may serve a response within **FORTY-FIVE (45)** days after service upon such Defendant of the Summons and Complaint or other documents nitiating the civil action.

The documents or things sought by this Request include documents and things in the possession, custody or control of the party or person, his attorney and all agents, servants, representatives, investigators and others who may have obtained custody of the documents and things on behalf of the opposing party or his attorneys.

Each party to whom this Request is directed seasonably to supplement his response with respect to any question directly addressed to the indentity and location of persons having knowledge of discoverable matters and the identify of each person expected to be called as an expert witness at the trial, the subject matter on which he is expected to testify and the substance of his testimony. Each party to whom this Request is directed is required seasonably to amend a prior response if he obtains information on the basis of which he knows that the response was incorrect when made or he knows that the response, though correct when made, is no longer true and the circumstances are such that a failure to amend a response is in substance knowing concealment.

Where the terms "you", "Plaintiff", "Defendant" or any other designation for a party are used, they are meant to include every individual party and separate responses should be given for each person named as a party, if requested. Where an individual request calls for a response which involves more than one item, the response of each party should be clearly set out so that it is understandable and so that the items are differentiated.

Each party upon whom this Request is served is hereby notified that should such party fail to comply with this Request or any part thereof, then the undersigned party may seek sanctions under **RCP 37(a)**.

COPIES MAILED pursuant to **RCP 5** this date to these persons, in these capacities and at these addresses:

Suite No. 490
Tempe, Arizona 85282
Attorneys for Defendants

DATED this _____ day of November, 1991.

EDWARDS & EDWARDS

By ______________________________
J. Stanley Edwards
10505 North 69th Street
Suite No. 800
Scottsdale, Arizona 85253
Attorneys for Plaintiff

ATTACHMENT "A"

The following definitions shall apply on all Request for Production contained herein:

1. "Communication" means any contact between two or more persons or companies or other entities or between any person and another entity and shall include, without limitations, written contact by such means as letters, memoranda, telegrams, telex or by any other document (as defined herein), or by oral contact such and such other means as face-to-face meetings, telephone conversations and any contact between persons involving computer interfacing.

2. The terms "concerning", "pertaining", "relating", "with respect to", "with regard to" and/or "regarding", as used herein, are interchangeable and include referring to, alluding to, responding to, connected with, commenting on, in respect of, about, discussing, showing, describing, mentioning, reflecting, analyzing, constituting, evidencing or any similar term.

3. "Plaintiff/Defendant and/or the requesting party or responsive party" mean the named litigants in this action and their predecessors, successors, subsidiaries, affiliates, employees, agents, servants, representatives, partners and the like, wherever located.

4. "Document" is used herein in its customary broad sense, and means any kind of printed, recorded, written, graphic or phtographic matter, including taperecordings, however printed, produced, reproduced, coded or stored, of any kind or description, whether or not sent or received, including originals, reproductions, facsimiles, drafts and both sides thereof, and including, without limitations: papers, books, accounts, letters, models, photographs, sketches, drawings, blueprints, objects, tangible things, correspondence, telegrams, cables, telex messages, memoranda, notes, notations, work papers, routing slips, intra- and inter-office communications to, between or among directors, officers, agents, partners or employees, transcripts, minutes, reports and recordings of telephone or other conversations or of interviews or of conferences or of committee meetings or of other meetings, affidavits, statements, summaries, opinions, court pleadings, reports, indices, studies, analyses, forecasts, evaluations, contracts, licenses, agreements, invoices, notebooks, entries, ledgers, journals, books of records of account, summaries of accounts, balance sheets, income statements, questionnaires, answers to questionnaires, statistical records, advertisements, brochures, circulars, bulletins, pamphlets, trade letters, desk calendars, appointment books, diaries, telephone logs, expense accounts, lists, tabulations, charts, graphs, maps, surveys, sound recordings, data sheets, computer tapes and discs, magnetic tapes, punch cards, computer printouts, data processing input and output, computer files, computer programs, computer program coding

sheets, microfilms, microfische, all other records kept by electronic, photographic or mechanical means, and things similar to any of the foregoing, regardless of their author or origin or any kind, however denominated by the the responsive party and each of them.

5. "Meeting" and "meetings" mean any coincidence or presence of two or more persons, whether or not such coincidence or presence was by chance of prearranged, formal or informal or in connection with some other activity.

6. "Person" means any natural person, firm, partnership, joint venture, corporation or any other legal entity.

7. "You" and "your" means the party to whom this Request for Production of Documents and Things is directed, as defined in Paragraph 3 of these Definitions, and each of their agents, employees, attorneys and all other persons acting or purporting to act on behalf of them.

ATTACHMENT "B"

The following instructions shall apply to all Request for Production contained herein.

1. In producing documents and things, indicate the paragraph and subparagraph to which a produced document or thing is responsive in such a manner that the requesting party may easily ascertain each paragraph and subparagraph to which the document or thing is responsive.

2. In producing documents or things, furnish all documents and things known or available to you, regardless of whether such documents or things are possessed directly by you or your directors, officers, agents, employees, representatives, investigators or by your predecessors, successors, parent companies or entities, partners, subsidiaries, divisions or affiliates or by your attorneys or their agents, employees, representatives or investigators.

3. If any requested document or thing cannot be produced in full, produce said document or thing to the fullest extent possible, specifying each reason for your inability to produce the remainder and stating whatever information, knowledge or belief you do have concerning the unproduced portion.

4. If any document or thing requested was at one time in existence but is no longer in existence, then so state, specifying for each document or thing:

(a) the type of document or thing;

(b) the type(s) of information contained therein;

(c) the date upon which it ceased to exist;

(d) the circumstances under which it ceased to exist;

(e) the identity of all persons having knowledge of the circumstances under which it ceased to exist; and

(f) the identity of all persons who have or had knowledge of the contents thereof.

5. This Request for Production is deemed to be continuing. If, after producing documents and things you obtain or become aware of any further documents, things or information responsive to this Request for Production, you are required to produce to the requesting party such additional documents and things, and/or provide them with such additional information.

6. Unless otherwise indicated, all such documents and things should be retained by you until the final disposition of this litigation.

7. All documents and things shall be numbered consecutively by responsive party.

8. File folders with tabs or labels identifying documents called for by this Request for Production must be produced intact with such documents.

9. Selection of documents from the files and other sources and the numbering of such documents shall be performed in such a manner as to insure that the source of each document may be determined, if necessary.

10. Documents attached to each other should not be separated.

11. In the event that you seek to withhold any document or thing or information on the basis that it is properly entitled to some limitation of discovery, you are instructed to use the following procedure:

A. You shall, during the period for production of documents and things, supply the requesting party with a numerical list of the documents and things for which limitation of discovery is claimed, indicating:

(a) the name of each author, writer, sender, or initiator of such document or thing, if any;

(b) the name of each recipient, addressee or party for whom such document or thing was intended, if any;

(c) the date of such document, if any, or, if no date appears on said document, an estimate thereof and so indicate as an estimate;

(d) the general subject matter as described on such document, or, if no such description appears, then such other description sufficient to identify said document; and

(e) the claimed grounds for limitation of discovery (e.g., attorney/client privilege).

B. The responsive party shall provide the requesting party with the numbers of those documents on the list which the requesting party seek to discover.

C. Subsequent to such designation by the responsive party, the requesting party shall file such documents with the Court under seal for the purpose of permitting the Court to examine such documents in a manner commonly referred to as "in camera" for the purpose of determining whether such limitation on discovery shall be applicable or not applicable.

12. In lieu of producing originals of documents responsive to this Request for Production, you may, at your option, submit legible copies or other reproductions of such documents provided that the reproductions or copies are identical duplicates of the original documents, that the original documents from which such reproductions or copies were made are retained by you until the final disposition of this litigation, and that where original documents were attached in a like manner. Where an original document and any copy or copies thereof differ in any way, please produce both the original document and any copies thereof which differ from the original.

Exhibit "A"
TO
PLAINTIFF'S REQUEST FOR PRODUCTION
OF DOCUMENTS TO DEFENDANTS

1. Photographs referred to in Defendant's Answer to Uniform Interrogatory No. 537(a).

2. Copies of any opinions, documents, correspondence and the like prepared by any of the individuals or entities indicated in Defendant's Answers to Uniform Interrogatory No. 541, specifically including Engineering Associates and/or Research.

STUDY GUIDE
CHAPTER FOURTEEN

1. What is the definition of product liability? (254)

2. What are the three theories of recovery? (254)
(a)

(b)

(c)

3. What are the three types of injuries that can be caused by defective products? (254)
(a)

(b)

(c)

4. How is economic loss defined? (254)

(a) Why is it important to distinguish between economic losses and property losses? (254)

(1) Do most courts allow recovery for pure economic loss in strict liability cases? (254)

(b) Is there a clear distinction between economic loss and property loss? (254)

5. What are the three types of defects plaintiffs typically allege? (255)

(a)

(b)

(c)

6. How does a manufacturing defect differ from a design defect? (255)

7. Explain how <u>MacPherson</u> illustrates the concept of manufacturing defect. (255)

8. How does <u>MacPherson</u> differ from <u>Henningsen</u>? (257)

9. Can manufacturing defects be found in anything other than man-made products? (257)

(a) Explain. (257)

10. What is the main issue in a design defect case? (257)

11. On the basis of what theories of recovery can a design defect case be brought? (258)

12. What is a state-of-the-art defense? (258)

(a) Does this defense necessarily absolve a defendant of liability? (258)

13. For what reason do plaintiffs like to point out that a defendant redesigned a product after the plaintiff was injured? (258)

(a) Why is such evidence generally inadmissible? (258)

14. What are the three categories of design defects? (258)

(a)

(b)

(c)

15. What is a structural defect? (258)

(a) Must a defendant use the most durable design available? (258)

16. What must a defendant consider in deciding whether to incorporate a particular safety feature? (258)

17. Why is a defendant's argument that its design is as safe as the competition's not necessarily a winning argument? (259)

18. Can a defendant escape liability by arguing that the dangerousness of the product was obvious? (259)

19. What is meant by "foreseeable misuse"? (259)

(a) How does this apply to the production of vehicles? (259)

(b) What is the balancing test used by the <u>Turner</u> court? (266)

(c) Would you conclude from <u>Turner</u> that adherence to industry custom will protect a defendant from liability? (266)

(d) What arguments have been raised regarding airbags in the context of crashworthiness? (266)

20. What does a court consider when deciding whether a warning is adequate? (266)

(a) What types of warnings are expected of drug manufacturers? (266)

(b) Does a manufacturer have a duty to warn if it neither knew nor should have known of the danger at the time the product was sold? (267)

(c) Are manufacturers the insurers of their products? (267)

(1) Are there any apparent exceptions to this general rule? (267)

(d) If the dangerousness of a product is obvious is the manufacturer absolved from any duty to warn? (267)

21. Can the manufacturer of a component part be found negligent for failure to use reasonable care? (267)

(a) In what circumstances can a manufacturer who uses defective components be found negligent for their use? (267)

22. Is a manufacturer liable if a retailer fails to inspect its products if it is obligated to do so? (267)

(a) When is the manufacturer absolved of such liability? (267-268)

23. When is a retailer obligated to inspect goods? (268)

(a) What if the retailer is a car dealer? (268)

24. Can lessors of goods be found negligent for failing to discover defects? (268)

(a) What about those who supply services and who sell real estate? (268)

25. What is the privity requirement and how does it relate to negligence cases involving defective products? (268)

(a) Can someone who merely uses a product and does not purchase it sue a manufacturer for its negligence? (268)

26. Can a plaintiff suing in negligence recover for property damage? (268)

(b) Can a plaintiff recover for pure economic loss? (268)

27. What two types of law are involved in breach of warranty claims? (269)

(a) How do the public policies of contract law compare to tort law? (269)

(b) In what types of cases are contract remedies appropriate? (269)

(c) In what types of cases are tort remedies appropriate? (269)

(d) How does the type of loss affect the determination of whether a tort or contract should be filed? (269)

28. What are the three ways an express warranty can be made? (270)
(a)

(b)

(c)

29. Why is a breach of express warranty claim like a strict liability claim? (270)

30. Can a plaintiff recover for breach of express warranty if he/she is not in privity with the seller? (270)

(a) What if he is only a user and not a purchaser of the product? (270)

(b) What can a plaintiff who is a purchaser but who suffers only economic damage recover? (270)

31. What are two commonly used implied warranties? (270)
(a)

(b)

32. Define a warranty of merchantability. (270)

33. What is the sealed container doctrine? (271)

34. Does the warranty of merchantability apply to food and drinks? (271)

(a) What about real estate? (271)

(b) What about used goods? (271)

35. What is a warranty of fitness for a particular purpose? (271)

36. For what things can a direct purchaser recover on the basis of implied warranty? (271)

37. For what things can a remote purchaser recover on the basis of implied warranty? (271)

(a) Can a remote purchaser recover for economic damages? (271)

(1) How should he/she go about recovering for such damages? (271)

38. Can breach of warranty claims be brought against retail dealers? (272)

(a) What about component manufacturers? (272)

(b) What about sellers of used goods? (272)

(c) What about lessors? (272)

(d) What about sellers of real estate and sellers of services? (272)

39. Why do some plaintiffs opt for strict liability rather than warranty claims? (272)

(a) In what instances is warranty preferable to strict liability? (272)

40. For what three reasons should manufacturers be strictly liable for their products? (272)

(a)

(b)

(c)

41. What are the arguments against strict liability? (273)

42. What is the relationship betwen J. Traynor's opinion in Greenman and the Restatement (Second) of Torts Sec. 402A? (273)

43. According to the Restatement what four elements must a plaintiff prove if he/she is alleging strict liability? (273)

(a)

(b)

(c)

(d)

44. Does Section 402A of the Restatement apply to the provision of services? (274)

45. According to the Restatement what constitutes a defective condition unreasonably dangerous? (274)

(a) What is the difference between the "consumer expectation" test and the "risk-utility" test? (274-275)

46. What else can create a defective condition other than the characteristics of the product itself? (275)

47. What is an "unavoidably unsafe" product? (275)

(a) Give an example of such a product. (275)

48. What was the causation problem in Sindell? (276)

49. Why is it sometimes difficult for a plaintiff to prove that a defect existed at the time the product left the manufacturer? (276)

(a) In what way can the principles of res ipsa loquitur be used to assist the plaintiff in this process? (276-277)

50. What categories of people can be strictly liable for the sale or production of defective goods? (277)

(a) Can the seller of used goods be held strictly liable? (277)

51. What categories of people can recover on the basis of strict liability? (277)

(a) What is the potential problem with bystanders? (277)

52. What damages can a plaintiff recover if he/she sues on the basis of strict liability? (278)

(a) Can such a plaintiff recover for economic losses? (278)

53. What defenses can be raised to a warranty claim? (279)

(a) How do courts generally handle cases in which the plaintiff misused a product? (279)

(1) How does that approach affect the plaintiff in terms of burden of proof? (279)

(b) What must a defendant do in order to disclaim an implied warranty of merchantability? (279)

(1) How does federal law affect the disclaiming of warranties? (279)

(c) What do sellers frequently do to limit a plaintiff's remedies? (279)

(1) Are these attempts at limitation enforced by the courts? (280)

54. Is contributory negligence a defense to strict liability? (280)

(a) How is this rule affected by the fact the plaintiff misused the product or used it in an abnormal fashion? (280)

(b) Will the plaintiff be able to recover if the plaintiff is the proximate cause of his/her own injuries along with the manufacturer? (280)

55. Is comparative negligence a defense to strict liability? (280)

56. Is assumption of risk a defense to strict liability? (280)

57. What statutes of limitations are applicable to product liabliity claims? (280)

58. What is a statute of repose? (280)

(a) When does it begin to run? (280)

(b) Why can a statute of repose create a problem for some plaintiffs? (280-281)

REVIEW QUESTIONS

1. Describe the differences between the three different ways in which a product can be defective.

2. Describe the three classifications of damages in product liability cases. Why is it necessary to make these classifications?

3. What factors would you consider when deciding whether to pursue a negligence, strict liability or warranty cause of action?

4. What are the differences between express and implied warranties?

5. What elements would a plaintiff relying on a strict liability theory have to prove?

6. What defenses might a defendant raise in a product liability case?

7. Make an outline of the subject matter covered in this chapter so that you can see the interrelationships between the topics.

PUTTING IT INTO PRACTICE

Your firm takes on a client that apparently contracted AIDS after having been transfused with blood. If your firm decides to sue the blood bank that provided the blood, consider whether the client would have a better chance of recovering on the basis of negligence, strict liability or breach of warranty.

KEY TERMS

Define the following:

Defective condition unreasonably dangerous

Defective warning

Design defect

Disclaimers

Economic loss

Express warranty

Foreseeable misuse

Implied warranty

Manufacturing defect

Privity

Statute of repose

State-of-the-art defense

Structural defect

Unavoidably unsafe product

Warranty of fitness for a particular purpose

Warranty of merchantability

The following is a sample notice of independent medical examination.

Phoenix, Arizona ~~85014~~

State Bar No. 0(

State Bar No.

Attorneys for Defendant

IN THE SUPERIOR COURT OF THE STATE OF ARIZONA

IN AND FOR THE COUNTY OF MARICOPA

MARC A A Single Man, Plaintiff, vs. BERNADETTE M. and JOHN DOE Wife and Husband, Defendants.	No. CV 90- **NOTICE OF INDEPENDENT MEDICAL EXAMINATION** **AMENDED**

TO: Plaintiff, Marc , and his Attorneys of Record

Defendant, Bernadette M. , hereby serves notice on the Plaintiff, Marc to appear at the offices of Dr. T. Jr., located at North 15th Avenue, on Thursday, January 23, <u>1992</u>, at 9:30 a.m. for the purpose of submitting to an independent medical examination pertaining to Plaintiff's injuries which are the subject matter of Plaintiff's Complaint herein.

. . .

. . .

. . .

RECEIVED
10 1991
EDWARDS & EDWARDS
ATTORNEYS AT LAW

Interrogatories, Depositions,
Requests for Admission/
Production of Documents,
Motion for Summary
Judgements,
GAS, Food, Lodging 5 MI

STUDY GUIDE
CHAPTER FIFTEEN

1. What intent is required to commit an intentional tort? (288)

(a) Must the tortfeasor intend to harm the plaintiff? (288)

(b) Is it enough that the tortfeasor knows with substantial certainty that a certain result will occur? (288)

(1) What if the consequences are highly likely but not substantially certain? (288)

(c) Is it possible that an intentional tort may also be a crime? (288)

2. What is the "transferred intent" doctrine? (288-289)

(a) Is this doctrine applicable if the defendant intends to commit one tort but ends up committing another? (289)

3. How is battery defined? (289)

(a) Must the contact be with a part of the plaintiff's body? (289)

(b) Must the defendant actually touch the plaintiff? (290)

(c) Must the plaintiff suffer pain or bodily damage? (290)

(d) What is meant by "offensive" contact? (290)

(e) Must the plaintiff be aware of the contact at the time it occurs? (290)

(1) Give an example.

(f) Is the defendant liable for unforeseeable consequences? (290)

4. How is assault defined? (290)

(a) What are two ways an assault can be committed? (290)

(1)

(2)

(b) Is the transferred doctrine applicable to assault? (290)

(c) Must the plaintiff be aware of the impending contact? (291)

(d) Must the plaintiff be afraid that he/she will be harmed by the defendant? (291)

(e) Must the defendant have the ability to carry out the threatened contact? (291)

(f) Can the plaintiff recover if he/she feared that someone other than himself/herself would be harmed by the defendant? (291)

(g) Can a plaintiff recover for assault due to threats of future harm? (291)

(h) Are words alone sufficient to constitute an assault? (291)

(i) At what point is an assault completed? (291)

5. Define false imprisonment. (291)

(a) Does the blocking of someone' path constitute false imprisonment? (292)

(b) Is a plaintiff required to subject himself/herself to physical harm in order to escape confinement? (292)

(c) Is the doctrine of transferred intent applicable to false imprisonment? (292)

(d) Can something other than physical force be used to confine a person? (292)

(e) Must the defendant aim his/her threats directly at the plaintiff? (292)

(f) Can threats of future harm constitute false imprisonment? (292)

(g) Must the plaintiff be aware of his/her confinement at the time it occurs? (292)

(h) How can a police officer rebut a claim of false imprisonment? (292)

(i) Explain how false imprisonment arises in the context of shoplifting. (292)

6. What are the two mental states that can exist for the tort of infliction of mental distress? (293)

(a) How does a state of "recklessness" compare to negligence? (293)

(b) What constitutes "extreme and outrageous" conduct? (298)

(c) Are insults and manipulations of others considered "extreme and outrageous"? (298)

(d) Are the sensitivities of plaintiffs taken into consideration? (298)

(e) Is the doctrine of transferred intent applicable? (298)

(1) What is the exception to this rule? (299)

(2) If someone intends to commit an assault, will his/her intent be transferred to the emotional distress he/she actually causes? (299)

(f) What is a plaintiff required to prove in terms of damages? (299)

(1) Must he/she prove some type of physical harm? (299)

(g) To what standard of care are common carriers and public utilities held? (299)

(1) Why?

7. How is trespass defined? (299)

(a) What intent is required under modern law? (299)

(b) Is a defendant liable even if his/her contact with the plaintiff's land is by mistake? (299)

(c) Can a trespass be committed indirectly? (300)

(1) Give an example.

(d) Is a defendant liable simply because he/she is aware that an object may enter the plaintiff's land even if he/she does not intend it to do so? (300)

(e) Is the entry of gases or particles on another's land considered trespass? (300)

(1) What about vibrations caused by blasting? (300)

(f) Is the entry of another's air space considered trespass? (300)

(g) Can someone who has been given permission to enter land be liable for trespass? (300)

(h) For what consequences is one who has committed trespass liable? (301)

8. Define trespass to chattels. (301)

(a) Is recovery allowed even if the deprivation of possession is temporary? (301)

(b) Does a claim exist if someone other than the owner was in possession at the time of the trespass? (301)

(c) What intent is required for this tort? (301)

(d) Is it a defense that the defendant thought the property was his/her own? (301)

(e) Is the plaintiff required to prove actual harm? (301)

9. What is the difference between trespass to chattels and conversion? (301)

(a) How is conversion similar to trespass to chattels? (301)

(b) What are the consequences to the defendant if a plaintiff chooses to sue for conversion rather than trespass to chattels? (301)

(c) What factors are considered by the courts in determining whether a conversion has been committed? (302)

(1)

(2)

(3)

(4)

(5)

(6)

(d) Why is it that a defendant who mistakenly but in good faith takes another's hat and loses it will be liable for conversion while someone who returns it two days after discovering his mistake will not? (302)

(e) Can conversion be committed by the removal of goods? (302)

(f) Is it considered conversion if someone transfers property to someone not entitled to the property? (303)

(g) Can intangible rights be converted? (303)

10. Is mistake by itself considered a defense to an intentional tort? (303)

(a) Is mistake implicated in some of the defenses used in reference to intentional torts? (303)

11. Is consent generally a defense to an intentional tort? (303)

(a) How can consent be implied? (303)

(b) How is it determined that the plaintiff did or did not consent? (303-304)

(c) In what situations can a plaintiff not give consent? (304)

(1) Under what conditions will consent be implied in an emergency situation? (304)

(d) Is consent given if the plaintiff is mistaken about some material fact? (304)

(1) What if the defendant induced the mistake? (304)

(2) In what way does this issue arise in the context of medical care? (304)

(e) Can a plaintiff consent to a criminal act? (304)

(f) Is consent voluntary if given under duress? (304)

(1) What if the threats are of future harm? (304)

(2) What if the threats pertain to economic duress? (304)

(g) What is the result if a defendant exceeds the scope of the consent given by a plaintiff? (304-305)

12. What are the two key issues in self-defense cases? (306)

(a) Must the defendant be harmed to raise this defense? (306)

(b) Can this defense be used if there was no actual threat to the defendant? (306)

(c) How much force can a defendant use? (306)

(d) Can a defendant use force against words alone? (306)

(e) Can a defendant use force to defend himself/herself against future harm? (306)

(f) Can force be used against an aggressor who is rendered helpless? (306)

(1) Can it be used in retaliation? (306)

(g) What constitutes deadly force? (306-307)

(h) When can you use deadly force to defend your home? (307)

(i) What are the two positions the courts have taken regarding the duty to retreat? (307)

(1)

(2)

(j) Can deadly force be used to prevent a felony? (307)

13. When can a defendant use force to defend another? (307)

(a) What are the two positions the courts have taken in situations when the defendant mistakenly believed his/her assistance was necessary? (307)

(1)

(2)

14. What must a defendant do before he/she can use force to defend his/her property? (308)

(a) When is a defendant justified in using force to defend property? (308)

(b) What was the holding of Katko v. Briney in reference to property owners using mechanical devices to defend their property? (308)

(c) What must a property owner do before he/she can use a non-deadly mechanical device? (308)

(1) Will that be sufficient if the mechanical device constitutes deadly force? (308)

15. Why is a defendant who uses force to defend his/her property given more latitude than one who uses force to regain possession of his/her property? (309)

(a) What three requirements must be met before this defense can be used? (309)

(1)

(2)

(3)

(b) What is the courts' justification for allowing property owners to use force rather than the courts to regain possession of property? (309)

(c) What happens if property owners are mistaken in their belief that someone has their property or that force is necessary to regain possession? (309)

(d) What limitations have been imposed on merchants who detain suspected shoplifters? (310)

16. What is the majority rule regarding the use of force by landlords to evict their tenants? (310)

(a) What is the rationale for this rule? (310)

(b) What are the exceptions to this rule? (310)

17. What is the difference between necessity and the other defenses? (310)

(a) What is the difference between "public" and "private" necessity? (310)

(1) What is the consequence of that difference in terms of damages? (310)

(b) In order to claim public necessity must the potential harm being avoided be severe? (310)

(c) How do the courts determine if the privilege of necessity is justified? (311)

(d) When is private necessity a complete defense? (311)

(e) Can someone use force to prevent another from exercising the privilege of necessity? (311)

REVIEW QUESTIONS

1. What must the plaintiff prove in order to recover for the following:

(a) Assault

(b) Battery

(c) False imprisonment

(d) Infliction of mental distress

(e) Trespass to land

(f) Trespass to chattels

(g) Conversion

2. What are the differences and similarities between battery and assault? Between trespass to chattels and trespass to land? Between trespass to chattels and conversion?

3. Under what conditions is one justified in using force to defend one's property, one's self or another? What about deadly force?

4. In addition to self-defense and defense of another or property, what defenses might one raise to an intentional tort claim? What would one have to prove for each of these defenses?

5. What is the difference between public and private necessity?

PUTTING IT INTO PRACTICE

Your neighbor's son takes your brother's car for a joy ride. Your brother wants to follow him and retrieve the car, forcibly if necessary. Advise your brother of what he can and cannot do in his pursuit of the errant thief. Tell him specifically what he must do to avoid being liable for assault, battery, false imprisonment and infliction of mental distress. What justification does your brother have for following your neighbor's child?

KEY TERMS

Define the following:

Assault

Battery

Chattels

Conversion

Extreme and outrageous conduct

False imprisonment

Intentional tort

Private necessity

Public necessity

Transferred intent

Trespass to chattels

Trespass to land

The following are sample jury instructions approved for use in Arizona. You should check to see if your state has approved jury instructions.

PERSONAL INJURY DAMAGES INSTRUCTIONS

Introduction

The Damages Instructions were in the Negligence Section of *RAJI (Civil)*. They have been incorporated into *RAJI (Civil)* 2d, with modifications. Since these damages instructions are appropriate for use in all personal injury cases, not just negligence cases, they are now in their own section.

In the typical personal injury case, the basic instructions are in the Standard Section, the case specific instructions are in the specialized section (Fault, Negligence, Medical Negligence, Product Liability), and the damages instructions are in the Personal Injury Damages Section.

Except for the punitive damages instruction, the Personal Injury Damages Instructions will not be useful without major modification in many Bad Faith or Contract cases. The Committee has therefore placed in the Bad Faith and Contract Sections some damages instructions drafted specifically for those types of cases.

PERSONAL INJURY DAMAGES 1

Measure of Damages

If you find [any] defendant liable to plaintiff, you must then decide the full amount of money that will reasonably and fairly compensate plaintiff for each of the following elements of damages proved by the evidence to have resulted from the fault of [any] [defendant] [party] [person]:[1]

(1) The nature, extent, and duration of the injury.

(2) The pain, discomfort, suffering, disability, disfigurement, and anxiety already experienced, and reasonably probable to be experienced in the future as a result of the injury.

(3) Reasonable expenses of necessary medical care, treatment, and services rendered, and reasonably probable to be incurred in the future.

(4) Lost earnings to date, and any decrease in earning power or capacity in the future.

(5) Loss of love, care, affection, companionship, and other pleasures of the [marital] [family] relationship.

SOURCE: *RAJI (Civil)* Negligence 10, as modified.

USE NOTE: [1]. Use the appropriate bracketed language, as follows:

(1) "defendant" — One defendant, no claim of plaintiff's fault.

(2) "any defendant" — More than one defendant, no claim of plaintiff's fault.

(3) "any party" — One or more defendants, claim of plaintiff's fault.

(4) "any person" — One or more defendants, claim of non-party fault (with or without a claim of plaintiff's fault).

(5) Alternatives: Any appropriate combination of the above; or, identify by name all those who might be at fault; or, simply say: ". . . resulted from any fault in the case."

2. **Modifications:** Depending on the evidence in the case, some of the elements in Paragraphs 2, 3, 4, and 5 may be inapplicable or cumulative, and some unlisted elements may be applicable and not cumulative. Customize the instruction to fit the case.

3. **Property Damage Claim:** If there is a property damage claim, add, as the last element of the instruction: "(6) The difference in the value of the damaged property immediately before and immediately after the damage."

PERSONAL INJURY DAMAGES 2

Pre-Existing Condition, Unusually Susceptible Plaintiff

Plaintiff is not entitled to compensation for any physical or emotional condition that pre-existed the fault of defendant. However, if plaintiff had any pre-existing physical or emotional condition that was aggravated or made worse by defendant's fault, you must decide the full amount of money that will reasonably and fairly compensate plaintiff for that aggravation or worsening.

You must decide the full amount of money that will reasonably and fairly compensate plaintiff for all damages caused by the fault of defendant, even if plaintiff was more susceptible to injury than a normally healthy person would have been, and even if a normally healthy person would not have suffered similar injury.

SOURCE: *California Jury Instructions, Civil (BAJI)* 14.65 (6th Ed.) as modified; *RAJI (Civil)* Negligence 10A, as modified.

USE NOTE: 1. **Identification of Possible Parties at Fault:** The instruction is drafted for a one-defendant, no comparative fault case. In other cases, replace "defendant" here with the same language used in *RAJI (Civil)* 2d Personal Injury Damages 1 from the "[any] [defendant] [party] [person]" options.

2. **The Two Principles Covered by this Instruction:** Use the first paragraph when there is an issue of aggravation of pre-existing condition. ("Worsening" has been added as a clarification of "aggravation"; some may find the instruction just as clear with one or the other of those concepts removed.) Use the second paragraph when there is an issue of injury to an unusually susceptible person. Use both paragraphs if both issues are in the case.

3. **"Fault" or "Negligence":** If desired, "negligence" can be substituted for "fault" in this instruction; the instruction will be correct either way.

PERSONAL INJURY DAMAGES 3

Damages for Wrongful Death of Spouse, Parent, or Child

If you find defendant liable to plaintiff, you must then decide the full amount of money that will reasonably and fairly compensate (name of each survivor) [separately] for each of the following elements of damages proved by the evidence to have resulted from the death of (name of decedent).

(1) The loss of love, affection, companionship, care, protection, and guidance since the death and in the future.

(2) The pain, grief, sorrow, anguish, stress, shock, and mental suffering already experienced, and reasonably probable to be experienced in the future.

(3) The income and services that have already been lost as a result of the death, and that are reasonably probable to be lost in the future.

(4) The reasonable expenses of funeral and burial.

(5) The reasonable expenses of necessary medical care and services for the injury that resulted in the death.

SOURCE: A.R.S. § 12-613; *RAJI (Civil)* Negligence 10B; *City of Tucson v. Wondergem*, 105 Ariz. 429, 466 P.2d 383 (1970); *Jeffery v. United States*, 381 F. Supp. 505 (Ariz. 1974); *Salinas v. Kahn*, 2 Ariz. App. 181, 407 P.2d 120 (1965).

USE NOTE: Depending on the evidence in the case, some of the elements in Paragraphs 1 and 2 may be inapplicable or cumulative, and the elements listed in paragraphs 3, 4, and 5 may be inapplicable. Customize the instruction to fit the case.

PERSONAL INJURY DAMAGES 4

Punitive Damages

If you find defendant liable to plaintiff, you may consider assessing additional damages to punish defendant or to deter defendant and others from similar misconduct in the future. Such damages are called "punitive" or "exemplary" damages.

To recover such damages, plaintiff has the burden of proving by clear and convincing evidence, either direct or circumstantial, that defendant acted with an evil mind.

This required state of mind may be shown by any of the following:

(1) Intent to cause injury; or

(2) Wrongful conduct motivated by spite or ill will; or

(3)[1] [Defendant acted to serve his own interests, having reason to know and consciously disregarding a substantial risk that his conduct might significantly injure the rights of others.]

[Defendant consciously pursued a course of conduct knowing that it created a substantial risk of significant harm to others.]

To prove this required state of mind by clear and convincing evidence, plaintiff must persuade you that the punitive damages claim is highly probable. This burden of proof is more exacting than the standard of more probably true than not true, which applies to all other claims in this case, but it is less exacting than the standard of proof beyond a reasonable doubt.

The law provides no fixed standard for the amount of punitive damages you may assess, if any, but leaves the amount to your discretion. [However, if you assess punitive damages, you may consider the character of defendant's conduct or motive, the nature and extent of the harm to plaintiff that defendant caused, and the nature and extent of defendant's financial wealth.][2]

SOURCE: 1. **Elements of Punitive Damages:** *RAJI (Civil)* Negligence 10C; *Linthicum v. Nationwide Life Ins. Co.*, 150 Ariz. 326, 723 P.2d 675 (1986); *Rawlings v. Apodaca*, 151 Ariz. 149, 726 P.2d 565 (1986); *Hawkins v. Allstate Ins. Co.*, 152 Ariz. 490, 733 P.2d 1073 (1987); *Gurule v. Illinois Mut. Life and Cas. Co.*, 152 Ariz. 600, 734 P.2d 85 (1987); *Volz v. Coleman Company, Inc.*, 155 Ariz. 567, 748 P.2d 1191 (1987); *Bradshaw v. State Farm Mut. Auto Ins.*, 157 Ariz. 411, 758 P.2d 1313 (1988).

2. **Definition of Clear and Convincing:** *State v. Renforth*, 155 Ariz. 385, 746 P.2d 1315 (App. 1987), *review denied*, 158 Ariz. 487, 763 P.2d 983 (1988); *State v. King*, 158 Ariz. 419, 422, 763 P.2d 239, 242 (1988). *See also*, *U.S. v. Owens*, 854 Fed. 2d 432, 436 (11th Cir. 1988), which accepted the *Renforth* definition of the clear and convincing standard of proof.

Punitive Damages

USE NOTE: [1] **Bracketed "State of Mind" Statements at Element 3:** Use the bracketed language most appropriate for the case. The first bracketed statement is taken directly from *Bradshaw*; the second is taken directly from *Gurule*. Although the bracketed statements cover the same principle, there are differences between the two. In some cases, therefore, one statement might be preferable to the other. Select one of the statements, but probably not both, as appropriate for the case. Or, replace both statements with other satisfactory language expressing the same principle. *See* Comment 1, *infra*.

[2] **Brackets:** The brackets around the last sentence of *RAJI (Civil)* 2d Damages 4 indicate that some of the factors listed could be deleted or others added, depending on the evidence in a particular case.

3. **Burden of Proof Paragraph:** The burden of proof contained in this instruction is for use when the only claim in the case requiring proof by clear and convincing evidence is for punitive damages. If the clear and convincing standard applies to both punitive damages and other kinds of claims in the case, delete the burden of proof paragraph here and use *RAJI (Civil)* 2d Standard 10. (In either situation, also use *RAJI (Civil)* 2d Standard 9.)

COMMENT: 1. **Alternative Definitions of Evil Mind:** Beginning with the 1986 cases of *Linthicum* and *Rawlings*, the Arizona Supreme Court has redefined the conduct, state of mind, and level of proof required for assessment of punitive damages. *RAJI (Civil)* 2d Personal Injury Damages 4 provides three alternative ways to show the "evil mind" element of a punitive damages claim. The specific language for these alternatives is directly from *Bradshaw*, (and *Gurule*).

The Committee does not suggest that the alternatives set forth in the instruction are exclusive of all others, or that they have been stated here in the *only* correct way. The Arizona Supreme Court opinions contain many statements and expressions discussing and defining "evil mind." The trial court may find other "evil mind" statements or formulations more appropriate for a particular case than any of those provided in Personal Injury Damages 4; in that event, the instruction may serve as a template.

2. **DUI or Other Voluntary Intoxication Cases:** If there is adequate evidence that plaintiff's injury resulted from defendant's driving while under the influence of intoxicating liquors, a punitive damages instruction is probably warranted. However, "intoxication alone, in the absence of other compelling circumstances, may not warrant punitive damages." *Olson v. Walker*, 162 Ariz. 174, 781 P.2d 1015 (App. 1989).

Punitive Damages

3. **New Punitive Damages Case:** There is a recent U.S. Supreme Court case on punitive damages: *Pacific Mutual Life Insurance Co. v. Haslip*, ___ U.S. ___, 111 S. Ct. 1032, 113 L. Ed. 2d 1 (1991).

In *Haslip*, the Supreme Court addressed a due process clause challenge to an Alabama jury's award of punitive damages. The majority, concurring, and dissenting opinions are lengthy. The *Haslip* majority held that constitutional due process requirements were met in the case because the jury instructions, the post-trial procedures, and the state appellate review procedures all combined to place reasonable constraints on the jury's discretion regarding punitive damages.

Haslip was announced too close to the *RAJI (Civil)* 2d publication deadline for the Committee to adequately reconsider the punitive damages instruction in light of *Haslip*. By this comment, the Committee does not mean to suggest that the *RAJI (Civil)* 2d Punitive Damages Instruction is inadequate. But, the Committee does suggest that court and counsel read and consider *Haslip* (and any progeny) before instructing on punitive damages.

PERSONAL INJURY DAMAGES 5

Mortality Tables and Life Expectancy

According to the 1987 *Vital Statistics of the United States*, a person aged ___ years has a life expectancy of ___ years. This is merely an estimate of the probable average remaining length of life of all persons of this age.

This estimate may be considered by you in determining the amount of damages for any permanent injury proved by the evidence to have resulted from the fault of [any] [defendant] [party] [person].[1]

SOURCE: *RAJI (Civil)* Standard 7, as modified.

USE NOTE: [1] Use the same bracketed options here as used in Personal Injury Damages 1.

COMMENT: Evidence of life expectancy has traditionally been admitted in Arizona. *See, e.g., Alabama Freight Lines v. Thevenot*, 68 Ariz. 260, 204 P.2d 1050 (1949). The 1967 MARJI instructions, the predecessors to RAJI, contained a life expectancy instruction. The cited source was: "Traditional Maricopa County Instruction." The MARJIs and RAJIs have always contained reference to the *Commissioner's Standard Table on Mortality*. But West Publishing Company no longer includes that table in its publication of the Arizona Revised Statutes. The most recent Commissioner's Table is the 1980 Table. The 1987 Life Tables in the *Vital Statistics of the U.S.* are more current. (Also, the *Commissioner's Table* is based on a survey of insured persons; the *Vital Statistics of the United States*, Life Tables are based on general population data.) The Committee recommends use of the *Vital Statistics of the United States*, Life Tables.

The 1987 Life Tables are the most recent available at time of publication. As new tables are published by the Department of Health and Human Services, they will be included in Supplements to *RAJI (Civil)* 2d. For convenience, *RAJI (Civil)* 2d includes a copy of the "All Races" 1987 Life Tables.

1987 LIFE TABLES[1]

Expectation of Life at Single Years of Age: United States, 1987, All Races

Age	Both Sexes	Male	Female	Age	Both Sexes	Male	Female	Age	Both Sexes	Male	Female
0	75.0	71.5	78.4	30	46.9	43.8	49.8	60	20.5	18.2	22.5
1	74.7	71.3	78.1	21	46.0	42.9	48.9	61	19.8	17.5	21.7
2	73.8	70.3	77.1	32	45.0	42.0	47.9	62	19.1	16.8	21.0
3	72.8	69.4	76.2	33	44.1	41.1	46.9	63	18.3	16.1	20.2
4	71.9	68.4	75.2	34	43.1	40.2	46.0	64	17.6	15.5	19.4
5	70.9	67.4	74.2	35	42.2	39.2	45.0	65	16.9	14.8	18.7
6	69.9	66.5	73.2	36	41.3	38.3	44.1	66	16.3	14.2	17.9
7	68.9	65.5	72.2	37	40.4	37.4	43.1	67	15.6	13.6	17.2
8	67.9	64.5	71.3	38	39.4	36.5	42.2	68	14.9	13.0	16.5
9	66.9	63.5	70.3	39	38.5	35.6	41.2	69	14.3	12.4	15.8
10	66.0	62.5	69.3	40	37.6	34.7	40.3	70	13.6	11.8	15.1
11	65.0	61.6	68.3	41	36.7	33.8	39.3	71	13.0	11.2	14.4
12	64.0	60.6	67.3	42	35.8	32.9	38.4	72	12.4	10.7	13.7
13	63.0	59.6	66.3	43	34.8	32.0	37.4	73	11.9	10.2	13.0
14	62.0	58.6	65.3	44	33.9	31.1	36.5	74	11.3	9.7	12.4
15	61.0	57.6	64.3	45	33.0	30.3	35.6	75	10.7	9.2	11.8
16	60.1	56.7	63.4	46	32.1	29.4	34.7	76	10.2	8.7	11.2
17	59.1	55.7	62.4	47	31.2	28.5	33.7	77	9.7	8.2	10.6
18	58.2	54.8	61.4	48	30.4	27.7	32.8	78	9.1	7.8	10.0
19	57.2	53.9	60.5	49	29.5	26.8	31.9	79	8.6	7.4	9.4
20	56.3	53.0	59.5	50	28.6	26.0	31.0	80	8.2	6.9	8.8
21	55.3	52.1	58.5	51	27.8	25.1	30.2	81	7.7	6.6	8.3
22	54.4	51.1	57.6	52	26.9	24.3	29.3	82	7.2	6.2	7.8
23	53.5	50.2	56.6	53	26.1	23.5	28.4	83	6.8	5.8	7.3
24	52.5	49.3	55.6	54	25.3	22.7	27.5	84	6.4	5.5	6.9
25	51.6	48.4	54.6	55	24.4	21.9	26.7	85	6.1	5.2	6.4
26	50.7	47.5	53.7	56	23.6	21.2	25.8				
27	49.7	46.6	52.7	57	22.8	20.4	25.0				
28	48.8	45.6	51.7	58	22.1	19.6	24.2				
29	47.8	44.7	50.8	59	21.3	18.9	23.3				

[1] National Center for Health Statistics. *Vital Statistics of the United States*, 1987, Vol. II, mortality, Part A. Section 6—Life Tables, page 11, Table 6-3. Washington: Public Health Service, 1990. (DHHS Publication No. (PHS) 90-1101.)

STUDY GUIDE
CHAPTER SIXTEEN

1. In basic terms what is misrepresentation? (319)

(a) How does misrepresentation relate to other torts? (319)

(b) How is misrepresentation related to the tort of deceit? (319)

(d) How does misrepresentation differ from deceit? (319)

(e) What is fraud? (319)

2. What are the three types of misrepresentation? (319)
(a)

(b)

(c)

3. What are the four elements of misrepresentation? (319)
(a)

(b)

(c)

(d)

4. Other than affirmatively making a false statement what are the ways in which misrepresentation can be committed? (319)

(a)

(b)

(c)

5. Under modern law when is nondisclosure of a material fact considered misrepresentation? (320)

(a) Can actions alone constitute misrepresentation? (319)

(b) Give an example of a situation in which a seller would be obligated to disclose a material fact to a buyer. (320)

(c) How does Universal Investment Co. v. Sahara Motor Inn illustrate this principle of disclosure? (320)

6. Can a defendant be found liable for misrepresentation if he/she makes a half-truth? (321)

7. What kind of obligation is imposed on a defendant as a result of sharing a fiduciary relationship with the plaintiff? (321)

8. When is a court most likely to find nondisclosure of a fact to be misrepresentation? (322)

9. Is a defendant liable only to those persons he/she intended to influence by a misrepresentation? (322)

(a) In what situations might a defendant be liable even if he/she did not intend to influence a particular plaintiff? (322)

(1)

(2)

(3)

10. Give an example of a situation in which a plaintiff might rely on the defendant's misrepresentation because the misrepresentation occurred in the type of transaction the defendant could reasonbly expect the plaintiff to engage in as result of his/her reliance on the misrepresentation. (322)

(a) Give an example of a situation in which plaintiffs could recover for misstatements made in commercial documents. (322)

11. What state of mind is required to prove intentional misrepresentation? (322)

(a) When can a defendant be liable for making a statement that is merely his/her belief? (322)

12. If a plaintiff makes an independent investigation of the defendant's representations, can the plaintiff still be deemed to have relied on the defendant's statements? (323)

13. In what circumstances is a plaintiff justified in relying on a defendant's opinion? (323)

(a)

(b)

(c)

14. Is "puffing" actionable as misrepresentation? (323)

15. Is a person justified in relying on an opinion offered by a "disinterested" party? (323-324)

(a) Give an example of when such reliance might be justified. (324)

16. Is one justified in relying on someone's opinion if the person offering the opinion implies there are no facts inconsistent with that opinion? (324)

17. Is the line between fact and opinion always a clear one? (324)

(a) When might a statement regarding value of an object be classified as fact rather than opinion? (324)

18. Are predictions typically regarded as opinions or facts? (324)

(a) When might a prediction be considered an opinion? (324)

19. Is an individual entitled to rely on another's statement regarding his/her intentions? (324)

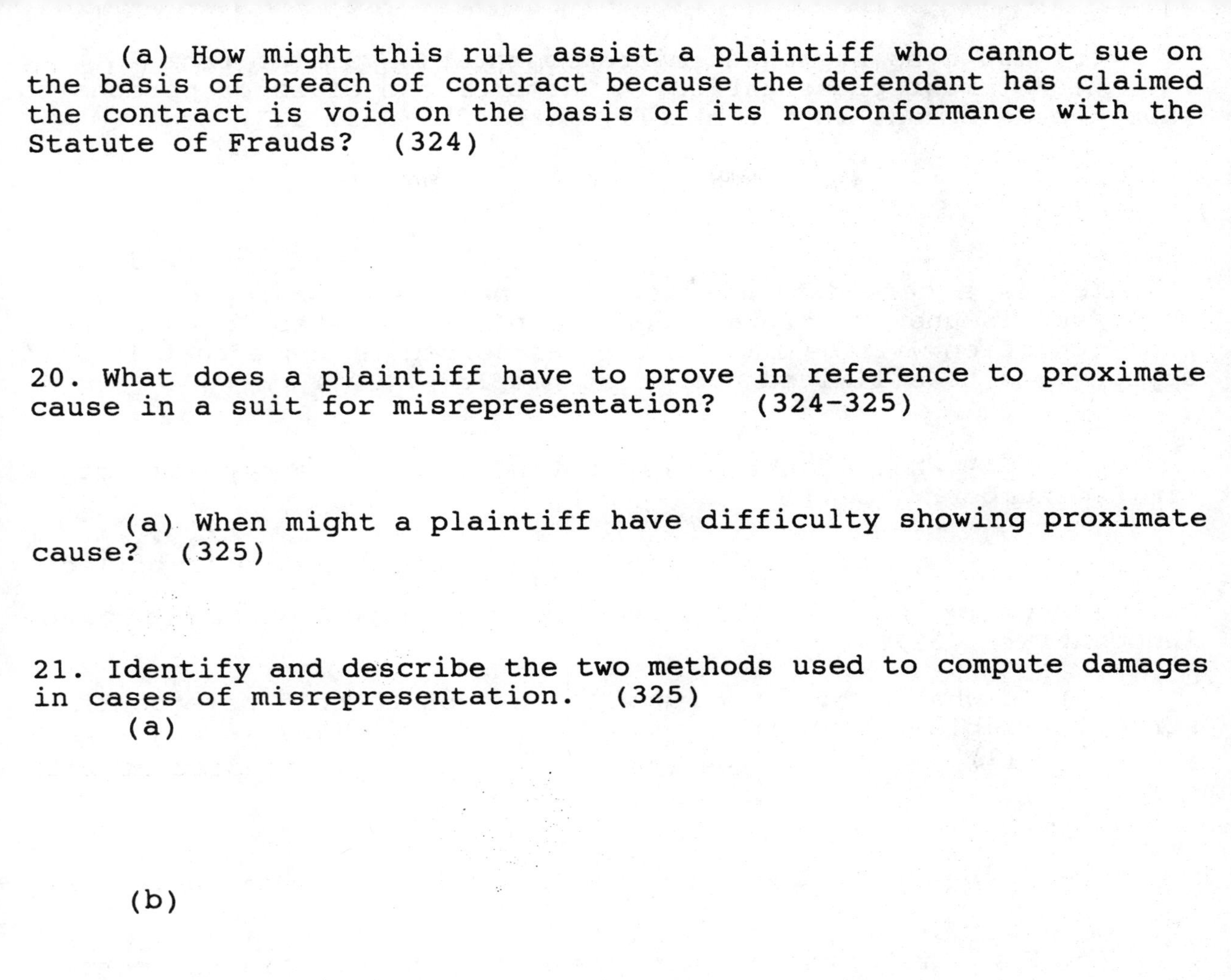

(a) How might this rule assist a plaintiff who cannot sue on the basis of breach of contract because the defendant has claimed the contract is void on the basis of its nonconformance with the Statute of Frauds? (324)

20. What does a plaintiff have to prove in reference to proximate cause in a suit for misrepresentation? (324-325)

(a) When might a plaintiff have difficulty showing proximate cause? (325)

21. Identify and describe the two methods used to compute damages in cases of misrepresentation. (325)

(a)

(b)

22. Have the courts always allowed recovery for negligent misrepresentation? (325)

(a) In what types of cases are the courts most likely to allow a claim for negligent misrepresentation? (325)

(b) Can a defendant be found liable for negligent misrepresentation if he/she received no direct compensation? (325)

(c) How does negligent misrepresentation differ from intentional misrepresentation in terms of the class of persons to whom the defendant is potentially liable? (325; 327)

(d) Is a defendant liable for a negligent misrepresentation if he/she is unaware of the identity of the persons to whom the representation will be made as long as he/she is aware that it will be conveyed to a limited number of people? (327)

(1) What if the people intended to be reached are not a limited number? (327)

23. Do the courts always allow recovery for misrepresentations made innocently? (327)

(a) In what circumstances will the courts hold defendants strictly liable for their misrepresentations? (327)

(1)

(2)

(b) How does innocent misrepresentation arise in the context of product liability? (327-328)

REVIEW QUESTIONS

1. What must a plaintiff who alleges intentional misrepresentation prove?

2. What constitutes a misrepresentation?

3. When is an individual justified in relying on another's misrepresentation?

4. What are the differences between intentional and negligent misrepresentation?

5. What are the two ways a plaintiff might compute his/her damages upon successfully proving misrepresentation?

PUTTING IT INTO PRACTICE

A real estate agent is a client of the firm for which you work. The agent made some representations to a potential buyer about the value of a house that the buyer eventually bought. The representations later turned out to be wrong and the buyer has now sued the agent for misrepresentation. The agent swears to you that he had no idea that his statements were erroneous and wants to know what you think the chances of a successful suit against him are. Explain to him what the plaintiff must prove depending on what type of misrepresentation she alleges he committed. What information will you need before you can assess the plaintiff's chances of prevailing?

KEY TERMS

Define the following:

Benefits of the bargain measure of damages

Deceit

Fiduciary relationship

Fraud

Latent defect

Patent defect

Reliance measure of damages

The following pages contain a sample deposition summary.

In Re American Continental Corporation/Lincoln Savings and Loan Securities Litigation, MDL Docket No. 834

SUMMARY OF THE DEPOSITION OF SONJA HARINGTON
VOLUME I
JANUARY 00, 1991

PAGE/LINE	SUBJECT MATTER	TEXT	REFERENCES
EXAMINATION BY MOLLY BURKE, ESQ:			
12 : 1 - 14 : 5	EDUCATION	Sonja Harington, who has never before been deposed, received a B.S. in Business Administration in Dec. 1981 from Colorado State University. She has had only 3 accounting courses and is not an accountant. She has taken courses through the educational programs with companies she has worked with, in the areas of appraisals, lending, investments, futures and options, and a senior finance class. She is currently enrolled at the Pacific Coast Banking School, which is a 3-year program out of Seattle.	COLORADO STATE UNIV. PACIFIC COAST BANKING SCHOOL
14 : 6 - 15 : 23	EMPLOYMENT Chronology	In March 1982, Harington joined the Federal Reserve Board of Kansas City. She worked out of their Denver branch in holding company supervision and "was responsible for supervising and examining bank holding companies in the Kansas City district." She left in March 1984 and in Jan. 1985 joined the FHLB San Francisco "as an assistant analyst on the regulatory side." In Apr. '85 she was promoted to analyst and in Apr. '86 to acting manager. In Sept. '88 she became an analytical manager, although it was more a title change, and also in September '88, she "became an assistant director supervisory agent." In Aug. '90 she was sent to the SFB as "an acting deputy director" to fill in for someone who had gone to Washington, and was "in charge of systems and services." It was more administrative than regulatory and she oversaw the human resources and MIS.	FEDERAL RESERVE BOARD KANSAS CITY FHLB-SAN FRANCISCO (passim)
15 : 24 - 16 : 16	Federal Reserve Board (Kansas City)	At the Federal Reserve Board of Kansas City, Harington "had a case load of bank holding companies that [she] was responsible for monitoring." Her primary responsibility was for the states of Wyoming, Montana, Colorado, and parts of New Mexico, Kansas and Nebraska. She participated as an exam team member or an EIC. The exams were of holding companies rather than the banks themselves.	FEDERAL RESERVE BOARD KANSAS CITY

PAGE/LINE	SUBJECT MATTER	TEXT	REFERENCES
48 : 9 - 51 : 17	Concerns Heightened During '86 Exam "Significant Violations In Lots Of Different Areas"	The SFB's "concerns were heightened during the '86 examination about management and management capabilities." There was apprehension because "they had made . . . misrepresentations with respect to their operating plans." Furthermore, the investment in the Nameless Broadcast stock was "a speculative venture." "But definitely whatever concerns [the SFB] may have had were much more significant after the '86 examination." There was a concern "about their ability to operate [Lincoln] in a safe and sound manner. They didn't have any policies and procedures. They weren't documentating what they were doing, there were significant violations in lots of different areas. They weren't correctly calculating their income." The concerns extended into "what they were up to in terms of the backdating of documents, filestuffing, some of the other things that [the SFB] found." Nothing anyone ever did or said caused Harington to change her concerns.	NAMELESS BROADCAST
51 : 18 - 55 : 14	Appraisals "Deficient"; Losses Identified	Harington doesn't know what was meant by the first full ¶ on p.8 of Ex. 706 that begins, 'In addition.' The SFB "had problems in the past with Lincoln's appraisals." During the 1984 exam there had been an issue regarding Lincoln's filing of two "affiliated transactions for the sale of real estate, where when the appraisals were reviewed they were found to be deficient and . . . there were losses identified in looking at those appraisals." The SFB "knew that some of [Lincoln's assets] were overstated clearly because [they] had found the losses." Lincoln represented to the SFB in their response to the '84 exam "that all their appraisal practices and problems and deficiencies were remedied." There were numerous findings during the 1986 exam "that deal with Lincoln's appraisal practices in accounting. Lincoln [was] required by regulation to obtain appraisals for loans, and there were cases where they had not." There were losses, deficiencies and practices "contrary to regulatory requirements."	
55 : 15 - 57 : 3	Regulatory Violations	During the 1984 examination Harington was of an opinion that Lincoln had violated regulations such as overstating the value of certain real property, improperly accounting for contributions to service corporations in order to boost its grandfathered level of direct investments, and exceeding levels of investment authorized by the DSL.	F.R. TUCK

PAGE/LINE	SUBJECT MATTER	TEXT	REFERENCES
232 : 1 - 235 : 6	"LINCOLN WAS IN FACT VERY INSOLVENT"	Other than the meeting with Tuck to discuss the SFB's concerns about the debt budget, Harington had no other contact with Witless Accounting. After the conservator was appointed and jurisdiction was returned to the SFB, an attempt was made to get the old audit work papers for Lincoln, though she's not sure about ACC. She's sure she would have reviewed the financial statements audited by Witless Accounting because the SFB did get copies. When a conservator was appointed, the SFB "found out that things weren't quite as they appeared to be, and that Lincoln was in fact very insolvent and things were very much different than they had been represented." In the 1986 examination the SFB had identified improper accounting, non-recognition of losses, and some various other things that were not reflected in the audited financial statements." The last audited financial statements issued by Witless Accounting were in 1987 and they worked on Lincoln in 1988, at some point in time toward the latter part of the year. It was more than a year's time between the last audited financial statement and the appointment of the conservator.	F.R. TUCK WITLESS ACCOUNTING
235 : 7 - 244 : 25	VIRTUALLY ALL INFORMATION ABOUT ACC CAME FROM SECURITIES FILINGS OR AUDITED FINANCIAL STATEMENTS	The SFB "looked at all of the information . . . the institution sent . . . and incorporated that as part of [their] review and decision-making process. . . . [T]o the extent that might have changed it, it was changed; if it didn't, . . . then it wasn't changed." If the information submitted wasn't sufficient to alter the SFB's determination, then they relied on their own conclusions. There were clearly other issues that the SFB didn't have an ability to independently assess, and they would rely solely on the information provided by ACC and/or their accountants. "[I]n connection with most of the stuff that was happening at the holding company level, [the SFB] never had an ability to . . . do an independent assessment." To that extent, "whatever information was prepared by the auditors and/or the institution . . . that was the information that [the SFB] had." The "income of the holding company was declining, [b]ut . . . the representations that were being made to [the SFB] at the time primarily by Randy Bigit and J.W. Wish were that . . . things were changing at the holding company and they were getting out of those old lines of business and into new lines of business." The projected financial statements were not audited financial statements, and Harington doesn't know to what extent Witless Accounting assisted in the debt budget.	RANDY BIGIT J.W. WISH WITLESS ACCOUNTING F.R. TUCK

STUDY GUIDE
CHAPTER SEVENTEEN

1. How is the term "nuisance" defined? (334)

(a) Can the term be defined precisely? (334)

2. What is the difference between public and private nuisance? (334)

3. What must a plaintiff prove in a public nuisance claim? (334)

(a) Must the defendant's conduct constitute a crime? (335)

(b) Is it sufficient that the plaintiff suffer the same damages suffered by the rest of the public? (335)

(c) What is the problem associated with the plaintiff's having to prove "particular damage"? (335)

4. What must a plaintiff prove in the case of private nuisance? (335)

(a) Must the plaintiff own the land on which the nuisance allegedly occurred?

5. What is the difference between a nuisance and a trespass? (335)

(a) Has a nuisance occurred if nothing enters the plaintiff's property? (335)

(b) Can a plaintiff recover on the basis of nuisance even if no substantial harm occurs? (335)

6. What constitutes substantial interference? (335)

(a) Why might an abnormally sensitive plaintiff have difficulty recovering on the basis of nuisance? (335-336)

7. Must a defendant intend to interfere with the plaintiff's use and enjoyment of his/her land? (336)

8. How do some courts determine if a defendant's conduct is unreasonable for purposes of a nuisance claim? (336)

(a) How does the Restatement (Second) determine the reasonableness of conduct? (336)

9. What two remedies can a plaintiff recover for nuisance? (336)

(a) What must the plaintiff prove in order to secure an injunction? (336)

10. What defenses can be raised by the defendant in a nuisance suit?

(a) What is meant by a plaintiff "coming to the nuisance"? (337)

(b) Give an example of someone who would be considered to have "come to the nuisance."

(c) Is "coming to the nuisance" a complete defense? (337)

11. How did the right to privacy evolve? (337)

12. What four torts make up invasion of privacy? (337)

(a)

(b)

(c)

(d)

13. What is the tort of appropriation? (338)

(a) Give an example. (338)

14. Define what is meant by "unreasonable intrusion." (348)

(a) Give an example. (348)

15. How does one commit public disclosure of private facts? (348)

(a) Give an example. (349)

(b) Has a tort been committed if the details publicized are published in a public report? (349)

16. What is the tort of false light? (349)

(a) What is the difference between false light and defamation? (349)

17. Under what circumstances can a plaintiff recover for alienation of affections? (349)

(a) How does alienation of affections differ from criminal conversation? (350)

(b) What is the status of the torts of alienation of affections and criminal conversation? (350)

(c) In what situations might a parent be able to recover for alienation of affections? (350)

18. What three torts constitute interference with business relations? (350)

(a)

(b)

(c)

19. How does one commit the tort of interference with existing contractual relations? (351)

(a) What must the plaintiff prove?

(b) Can the defendant's interference be passive? (351)

(c) Can a plaintiff recover if the contract breached is an illegal one? (351)

(d) Can an at-will employee recover for this tort? (351)

(e) Can a plaintiff that has entered into a contract that is unenforceable because it violates the Statute of Frauds recover? (352)

(f) For what types of harm can a plaintiff recover for contractual interference? (352)

(g) Can a plaintiff recover if the defendant was breaching the contract to protect his/her own existing contractual rights? (352)

(h) Can a plaintiff recover if the defendant was breaching the contract in order to support some social interest? (352)

20. What is the difference between interference with existing contractual relations and interference with prospective contractual relations? (352)

(a) Give an example of how this tort can be committed by interfering with a plaintiff's nonbusiness expectations of financial gain. (352-353)

21. What is injurious falsehood? (353)

(a) What are the two types of injurious falsehood? (353)
(1)

(2)

22. What must a plaintiff who is alleging trade libel prove? (353)

(a) How does the tort of trade libel compare to defamation? (353)

23. Give an example of slander of title. (353)

24. What are the three torts that fall under the category of misuse of legal process? (353)

(a)

(b)

(c)

25. Who is the plaintiff in a suit involving misuse of legal process? (354)

26. How does one commit malicious prosecution? (354)

(a) What must the plaintiff prove? (354)

(b) In what situations would a proceeding be deemed <u>not</u> to have concluded in favor of the plaintiff? (354)

(c) What is the most difficult thing a plaintiff has to prove when alleging malicious prosecution? (354)

(d) What types of people are immune from malicious prosecution suits? (355)

27. How does malicious prosecution compare with wrongful institution of civil proceedings? (355)

(a) Give an example of an act that would be considered wrongful institution of civil proceedings. (355)

(b) Is it easier to prove lack of probable cause in a malicious prosecution case or in a wrongful institution of civil proceedings case?

28. Define the tort of abuse of process. (355)

(a) Give an example of abuse of process. (355)

(b) Is is sufficient for the plaintiff to show that the defendant had some ulterior motive for instigating a proceeding? (355)

REVIEW QUESTIONS

1. What is the difference between public and private nuisance? What are the elements of each tort?

2. What are the various ways a plaintiff might prove invasion of privacy and what are the differences among each of these torts?

3. What torts involve interference with family relations?

4. What are the various ways a plaintiff might allege interference with business relations and what would the plaintiff have to prove for each of these torts?

5. What tort claims might a plaintiff bring if he/she wanted to allege misuse of legal process and what would the plaintiff have to prove in each case?

PUTTING IT INTO PRACTICE

Suppose a client of your firm complains that her ex-husband, who lives in the same neighborhood as she does, continues to harass her by doing annoying and, in some cases, damaging things. Sometimes he opens her mail. At other times he walks back and forth on the sidewalk in front of her house, fully aware that she has clients that she is working with. On some occasions he has cornered her customers as they come out of her house and told them about other vendors that, according to him, are cheaper and more reliable than she is. Furthermore, he repeatedly threatens to call the police and tell them that she stole some expensive jewelry that he claims to belong to him even though she says he is fully aware that the jewelry is hers. What advice can you give her in terms of what torts her ex-husband might be committing?

KEY TERMS

Define the following terms:

Abuse of process

Alienation of affections

Appropriation

At-will employee

Criminal conversation

False light

Injurious falsehood

Interference with existing contractual relations

Inteference with prospective contractual relations

Malicious prosecution

Private nuisance

Public disclosure of private facts

Public nuisance

Slander of title

Trade libel

Unreasonable intrusion

Wrongful institution of civil proceedings

The following pages represent a report made as a result of an independant medical examination.

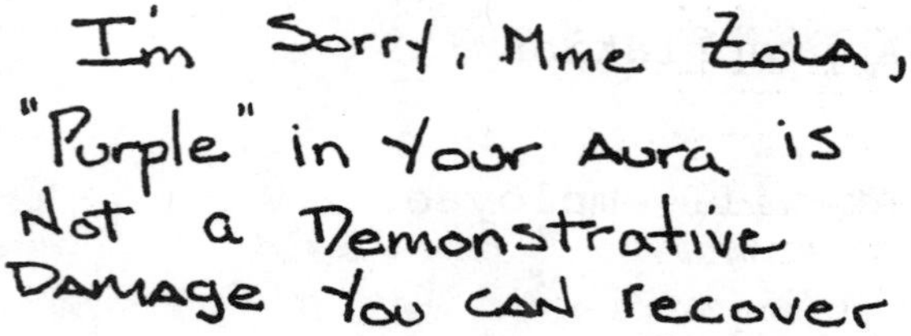

PHOENIX, ARIZONA 85015

RTHOPEDIC SURGERY

PHONE

January 23, 1992

To Whom It May Concern:

Re: Mark

This is to certify that Mark was seen in this office on 1/23/92 for orthopedic evaluation.

The patient's history begins on either the 20th or 21st of January, 1989, when he was in a car accident. He was the driver of a mid-sized car. A lady in a pickup of mid-size turned left in front of me as I was going down the road. He came to a dead stop eventually. No unconsciousness occurred but he doesn't remember too much at first. When he was hit, he states the pickup which was her car, spun around and hit me and then hit again, and he jumped over the curb, coming to a stop. His seat belt with shoulder strap was attached. His face was black and blue and ballooned out. His left knee hurt and his neck and low back hurt. Ambulance took him to Humana Hospital, Desert Valley. He was checked over, x-rays were taken and he was there about 5 or 6 hours and released home. Following this, he went to a chiropractor after a few days. Adjustments were done but he didn't think they did too much good to his neck and low back. Then he went to Dr. Pirie. A lot of physical therapy was done for his neck and his low back and he used the gym for a long time. For his left knee, some ultrasound was done and that didn't work. Then he went to Dr. an orthopedist. Anti-inflammatories were prescribed and he wore a brace for about a month and a half. Eventually he had an arthroscopic surgery and it was found that he had two bone chips under his kneecap as he understands it. Following the surgery he did his own exercises and worked it out. He improved some. He was last seen eight or nine months ago with Dr. He is due for one more checkup with Dr. Surgery was about a year ago. Dr. saw him right after the accident and told him he would be fine, he says.

Now reports that his neck and low back are all right. He has soreness once in awhile in the low back if he does any lifting but he can handle it, he reports. Otherwise he does all right. His knee at work, when he is walking or doing much working with weight bearing bothers him. He ran a race once time and the next day he couldn't move his knee. If he overdoes, it hurts. The race that he ran was about 1/8th of a mile. If he kneels or bangs his knee, it swells up pretty quick. Once in awhile the knee gives out. That is a little better and getting better. He still works with light weights but heavy weights bother him. No noises are noted.

PAST HISTORY: Right handed, no known drug sensitivities. No medical problems. No arthritis, bursitis or tendinitis. There was a broken bone in the left arm with no permanent problem at about age 15 or 16. No bone or joint or problems. Negative gastrointestinal history. Medicines don't upset his stomach. Nine months after this accident, he was rear-ended when he was riding his motorcycle and it snapped his neck. He saw Dr. . He got some treatment and recovered. His job is working in masonry.

Physical examination reveals a cooperative male who reports he is 5'10", weighs 180 pounds and is 22 years of age. His affect is normal.

Examination of the lumbar spine reveals normal contour. Gait pattern is normal without complaint. Toe and heel walking is accomplished without complaint. Flexion brings the fingertips to within two inches of the floor with pulling noted at the lumbosacral level. Extension is to 45 degrees with tightness only. Lateral bending is to 30 degrees without complaint. Bilateral rotation is to 30 degrees without complaint. From the ASIS, both lower extremities are 34-3/4 inches. Straight leg raising is easily to 70 degrees without complaint. Hip motion is normal without complaint. Mild tenderness is noted at L4 interspace. No other tenderness or muscle spasm is noted. No trigger points are noted. Straight leg raising in the sitting position is without complaint and without restriction on the right. On the left there is no restriction. There is mild discomfort in the left knee.

Examination of the cervicothoracic spine reveals normal contour. Lateral rotation brings the chin to within two inches of the supraclavicular fossa in either side. Flexion touches the chin to the anterior chest. Extension is to 30 degrees. Lateral bending is to 45 degrees. None of the cervical motions produce complaints. Full abduction of the upper extremities occur and the thumbs come from below posteriorly to the thoracolumbar juncture. There is no tenderness in the cervical, suprascapular, upper thoracic areas. No trigger points are elicited. Radial pulses are palpable. Adson maneuvers are negative.

A full range of motion of the left knee is present. The contour is present. There is no swelling. There is tenderness medially and laterally over the lower borders of the patella. There is mild crepitus in the inferior aspect of the patella. Extension and flexion produces some mild crepitus. Ligamentous stability is normal. There is no effusion. Lachman's test is negative. Patellar tracking is normal. The punctate scars are noted.

Neurological examination in the upper extremity reveals biceps reflexes 2+, triceps 2+, brachioradialis 2+. Pin prick response is normal. No intrinsic atrophy or weakness noted. Pin prick response is normal. No intrinsic atrophy or weakness is noted. Pinch tests are normal. Grip in the hands is equal. In the lower extremities, patellar reflexes are 2+. Hitting the patellar tendon on the left hurts, he reports. The Achilles are 2+. Posterior tibials are 2+, pin prick response is normal. No motor weakness is elicited. Muscle tone is good. Quadriceps tone is good.

Medical records are present and reviewed. X-rays from Humana Hospital on 1/28/89, date of injury, of the cervical, dorsal and lumbar spines are reported as normal. The chest x-ray is reported as normal. The EMS report is reviewed. The emergency room report indicates mild head trauma/acute. Cervical, thoracic and lumbar strains. Dr. records are reviewed. Initial evaluation is on 3/1/89. Nine diagnoses are listed. Physical therapy and OMT treatments are outlined and medication is prescribed. The follow-up reports are reviewed. Dr. report of 11/3/89 is reviewed concerning the motorcycle accident of October, 1989. Three diagnoses are listed and are mostly related to the cervical spine and headache. Comment is made concerning the proportion of contribution of each accident. On 11/5/90 a final report is rendered concerning the accident of 1/28/89. Patient is discharged from the doctor's care but recommendation is made for some continued treatment. Permanent impairment is listed as none. Dr. records of his initial evaluation of 5/23/90 is reviewed. Bipartite patella is noted. There are two ossicles at the tibial tubercle level, unchanged in position. Interesting impressions are noted in recommendations. Follow-up reports are reviewed. On 10/10/90 he reports the patient is getting along satisfactorily and he will see him back for probable final evaluation. Dr. report of surgery at Scottsdale Memorial Hospital on 9/13/90 is reviewed. Pre and postoperative diagnosis is (1) left knee fat pad impingement syndrome (2) Proximal patellar tendinitis (3) Symptomatic left tibial tubercle ossicles. The operative procedure is left knee arthroscopy with debridement of pad, open excision of loose tibial ossicles and debridement of patellar tendon. Dr. four page report of chiropractic care dated 11/28/90 is reviewed. His office records are concerned. Dr. letter of 1/18/91 is reviewed. He predicts that some continued pressure over the knee with kneeling or prolonged squatting activities. He does not feel any further surgery will be necessary. His report of 10/15/91 is reviewed.

COMMENTS: After examining the patient and reviewing the records, it is my opinion he sustained a left knee contusion and sprain, and sprain of his cervical and lumbar spine. After treatment he reports that his neck and low back symptoms have resolved. He has a few subjective symptoms without objective findings in his knee. He has a good result from the surgical procedure. It is my opinion that the patient's condition is stationary medically in relation to the injury of 1/20/89. He does not require any further treatments or examinations. In my opinion he has recovered from the effects of the injury of 1/20/89 with no evidence of permanent physical impairment attributable to the cervical or lumbar spines or to the left knee. The only positive findings on the left knee are related to the scars. His prognosis for the future is good. He can be normally active without medical restrictions.

M. D.

THT/deps

STUDY GUIDE
CHAPTER EIGHTEEN

1. How is vicarious liability defined? (363)

2. Name three circumstances in which a party may be vicariously liable. (363)

(a)

(b)

(c)

3. What is the doctrine of "respondeat superior"? (363)

(a) What is the rationale for this doctrine? (364)

(b) What is the practical reason underlying this doctrine? (364)

(c) Under what circumstances is this doctrine applicable? (364)

(d) Is an employer vicariously liable for the intentional torts of an employee? (364)

(e) Is an employer vicariously liable for injuries caused by an employee going to or from work? (364)

(f) Is an employer vicariously liable for injuries caused by an employee while on a "frolic" or "detour"? (364-365)

(g) How does the traditional view of "frolic" and "detour" differ from the more modern view? (365)

(h) Is an employer vicariously liable if he explicitly forbids an employee to do something and he does it anyway? (365)

(i) If an employee delegates his authority or rights to another without the employer's authorization, is the employer vicariously liable for the negligence of the third person? (365)

4. Is an employer vicariously liable for the negligent acts of an independent contractor? (365)

(a) What is the difference between an independent contractor and an employee? (365)

(b) What factors should be taken into consideration in deciding whether an individual is an employee or an independent contractor? (366)

(1)

(2)

(3)

(4)

(c) Is the fact that an employer refers to someone as an independent contractor dispositive in determining the nature of the relationship? (371)

5. Name and describe five exceptions to the non-liability rule regarding the vicarious liability of employers in reference to independent contractors. (371-372)

(a)

(b)

(c)

(d)

(e)

6. Historically what was the rule in reference to physicians' liability for those who worked under them? (372)

(a) What was the impetus behind this rule? (372)

(b) How has this rule changed in recent times? (372)

7. What is the difference between a bailor and a bailee? Give an example of each. (373)

(a) Under the common law is a bailor vicariously liable for the negligence of a bailee? (373)

(b) What if the bailor negligently entrusts control of his property to a person who he knows or reasonably should know is likely to endanger others? (373)

(c) For what reason have the courts typically side-stepped the non-liability rule for bailors in the context of vehicles? (373-374)

(d) What is the consequence if a court creates a presumption that an owner has control over his car? (374)

(1) Do all courts create such a presumption? (374)

(2) Is this presumption applicable if the owner is not present when the accident occurs? (374)

8. What is the family purpose doctrine? (374)

(a) Who created this doctrine and why? (374)

(b) Is this doctrine applicable even if the driver is using the car for his own purposes? (assuming the driver is a member of the owner's household and has permission to use the car) (374)

(c) What is the status of this doctrine today? (374)

(d) For what practical reasons do plaintiffs turn to this doctrine? (374)

9. Who created the automobile consent statutes and why? (374)

(a) What do these statutes provide? (374)

(b) Is the doctrine applicable if the bailee exceeds the scope of the bailor's consent? (374)

(c) Is the bailor still liable if the bailee loans the vehicle to a third person? (374)

(d) How has the "omnibus clause" affected the use of these statutes? (374)

10. What are the four elements of a joint enterprise? (375)

(a)

(b)

(c)

(d)

11. For what reasons is a social trip not considered a joint enterprise? (375)

12. What are the legal consequences of characterizing an activity as a joint venture? (375)

(a) In what types of circumstances does this doctrine normally arise? (375)

(b) How can this doctrine be used to prevent a passenger from suing the driver of the vehicle in which the passenger was riding? (375)

13. What does it mean if the negligence of one person is imputed to another? (376)

(a) What are the consequences of having the negligence of one spouse imputed to the other spouse? (376)

(b) What is the modern rule regarding the imputing of contributory negligence? (376)

(c) Give an example of a situation in which the contributory negligence of one party would be imputed to another. (376)

(d) Why is the negligence of a driver generally not imputed to a passenger in that same vehicle? (376)

(e) Why is the imputed negligence doctrine applicable when derivative claims are involved? (376)

14. Why have some states adopted statutes holding parents liable for the tortious acts of their children? (377)

(a) In what situations can parents typically be found liable? (377-378)

REVIEW QUESTIONS

1. In what circumstances is an employer vicariously liable for the acts of an employee?

2. In what circumstances is an employer vicariously liable for the acts of an independent contractor?

3. In what circumstances are parents liable for the acts of their children?

4. What are the exceptions to the bailor nonliability rule?

5. Give an example of a situation in which negligence would be imputed and contrast that with a situation in which negligence would not be imputed.

PUTTING IT INTO PRACTICE

You and a co-worker are involved in a motor vehicle accident. If the driver of the other vehicle wants to recover for her damages will she be able to sue your employer, whose car your co-worker was driving at the time? Will you be able to recover from the other driver for your damages? Are there any circumstances in which the driver of the other vehicle might be able to recover from you?

KEY TERMS

Automobile consent statute

Bailee

Bailor

Family purpose doctrine

Imputed negligence

Independent contractor

Joint enterprise

Respondeat superior

Vicarious liability

The following pages are a sample motion to compel filed in federal court.

Post Office Box
Phoenix, Arizona

Attorney State Bar No.
Attorney State Bar No.
Attorney State Bar No.

Attorneys for Defendant Mark R.
and Beverly Anne

UNITED STATES DISTRICT COURT

DISTRICT OF ARIZONA

JOHN J. and VIRGINIA M. husband and wife, Plaintiffs, v. et al., Defendants.	No. PHX WPC MARK MOTION TO COMPEL PRODUCTION OF DOCUMENTS AND STATEMENT PURSUANT TO D. ARIZ. 11(b)

Pursuant to Federal Rules of Civil Procedure 37(a) and 34(b), Defendant Mark moves to compel plaintiffs to produce their attorney's notes--and any other record--of a telephone call their counsel had with Mark before Mr. retained counsel.

Pursuant to District of Arizona Rule 11(b), counsel for Mark has attempted (as reflected in the correspondence attached as Exhibit A) personal consultation and sincere efforts to obtain the document at issue, but efforts have been unsuccessful.

This motion is supported by the attached memorandum. Mr. requests that this Court order plaintiffs to produce the relevant documents within ten (10) days and award the costs and attorneys' fees necessary in bringing this motion, pursuant to Rule 37(a)(4).

December 6, 1991.

By__

Post Office Box
Phoenix, Arizona

Attorneys for Defendant Mark R. and Beverly Anne

Copy mailed on December 6, 1991 to:

J. Stanley Edwards
Edwards & Edwards
Suite 800
10505 North 69th Street
Scottsdale, Arizona 85253

Delaine K McCarty

CIV 91-833 PHX WPC

October 11, 1991

Dear Tom:

Thank you for your letter of October 8. Because I have not seen your notes of any conversation with Mr.   and because it is still very early in the litigation, I cannot agree not to list you as a witness in this litigation.

Moreover, my request is that you provide us with <u>all</u> records of any conversation with Mr.   , including not just contemporaneous records (notes, memoranda, tape recordings, etc.), but also any subsequent documents that mention, cite to, or in any way rely upon that conversation.

I believe that our entitlement to those documents is clear, and if you are unwilling to provide them to us without conditions, we will move to compel their production.

Sincerely yours,

Michael

TELECOPIED

HMC:dg

ATTORNEY AT LAW

October 16, 1991

Re:

Dear Michael:

As I informed you in my letter of October 8, 1991, the only recorded memorandum of my telephone conversation with Mark R. is one page of hand-written notes taken down at the time of the call on January 11, 1991. There are no other records of the conversation and in response to your October 11 letter, there are, to the best of my knowledge, no "subsequent documents that mention, cite to, or in any way rely upon that conversation."

I continue to believe that you are not entitled to the personally prepared notes of my conversation with Mr. on January 11.

Sincerely,

TAL/at

LAW OFFICES

ATTORNEY AT LAW

October 8, 1991

Re:

Dear Michael:

This responds to your letter to me dated October 4, 1991 concerning your review of plaintiffs' responses to request for production.

The memorandum referred to by you is comprised of one page of handwritten notes of a telephone call made to me by Mark on January 11, 1991, after I had left word at his office on a prior day. My call to Mr. obviously occurred long before Mr. was considered a potential defendant in the present litigation and was made after witnesses for the plaintiffs in the state court litigation referred me to Mr. as a possible source of information in that case. Consequently, we believe these notes of mine are protected by the attorney work product doctrine.

Without waiving plaintiffs' rights to withhold any other documents, we are willing to give a limited waiver as to this memorandum of phone conversation, provided that it is agreed that I shall not be listed as a witness in this case. Upon your assurance of that, I shall make the memorandum available to you.

Sincerely,

TAL/at

October 4, 1991

Dear Tom:

In reviewing your responses to request for production, I noticed that you refer to a memorandum of a telephone conversation between one of the plaintiffs' attorneys and Mark [Response No. 4] Please send me a copy of that memorandum, together with any notes of the conversation, or any tape recording or other transcription or record of that conversation. To the extent that any of those things purport to reflect what Mr. said, I believe I am entitled to see them, regardless of whether you claim the protection of the work product doctrine.

Sincerely yours,

Michael

TELECOPIED

HMC:dg

Copy to:

J. Stanley Edwards, Esq.
Edwards & Edwards
10505 North 69th Street, Suite 800
Scottsdale, Arizona 85253

Attorney State Bar No.
Attorney State Bar No.
Attorney State Bar No.

Attorneys for Defendant Mark R.
and Beverly Anne

UNITED STATES DISTRICT COURT

DISTRICT OF ARIZONA

JOHN J. and VIRGINIA M. husband and wife, et al., Plaintiffs, v. et al., Defendants.	No. PHX WPC D. ARIZ. R. 11(K) STATEMENT IN SUPPORT OF MOTION TO COMPEL

Plaintiffs' responses to requests Nos. 4 and 12 of First Request for Production of Documents are deficient for the following reasons:

1. <u>REQUEST NO. 4</u>: Each and every document reflecting, evidencing, memorializing or otherwise relating to any conversation or communication between any Plaintiff or other person and Mark

<u>PLAINTIFFS' RESPONSE TO REQUEST NO. 4:</u> Plaintiffs have no knowledge of any document responsive to this request, except a memorandum of a telephone conversation between one of the attorneys for the plaintiffs and Mark that occurred prior to the filing

of the complaint in this action, which memorandum is privileged as attorneys' work product.

<u>REASON RESPONSE IS DEFICIENT</u>: Plaintiffs have failed to produce documents in their custody and control that are responsive to First Request for Production of Documents, such as the memorandum of a telephone conversation between one of the attorneys for the plaintiffs and Mark . Instead, plaintiffs have refused--and continue to refuse--to comply with their discovery obligations. The work product privilege will not protect the notes taken of a conversation with Mark because they are discoverable under the party statement exception to the work product rule. Even if protected by the work product privilege, substantial need and undue hardship exist to require production.

2. <u>REQUEST NO. 12</u>: All original or recorded statements of witnesses or persons with knowledge of any of the facts that are the basis of this litigation.

<u>PLAINTIFFS' RESPONSE TO REQUEST NO. 12:</u> Plaintiffs object to this request as calling for matters that are privileged as attorneys' work product. Without waiving this objection, plaintiffs have attached to this Response pages 112-114 of a transcript of the testimony of Richard before the U.S. Securities and Exchange Commission on March 8, 1991, and will provide the entire transcript to the Bank upon payment by it of plaintiffs' cost of the document, which is $600.00, the reporter's charge.

<u>REASON RESPONSE IS DEFICIENT:</u> Plaintiffs have failed to produce documents in their custody and control that are responsive to First Request for Production of Documents, such as the memorandum of a telephone conversation between one of the attorneys for the plaintiffs and Mark Instead, plaintiffs have refused--and continue to refuse--to comply with their discovery

obligations. The work product privilege will not protect the notes taken of a conversation with Mark because they are discoverable under the party statement exception to the work product rule. Even if protected by the work product privilege, substantial need and undue hardship exist to require production.

December 6, 1991

By__

Post Office Box
Phoenix, Arizona

Attorneys for Defendant Mark R.
and Beverly Anne

Copy mailed on December 6, 1991 to:

10505 North 69th Street
Scottsdale, Arizona 85253

Attorney State Bar No.
Attorney State Bar No.
Attorney State Bar No.

Attorneys for Defendant Mark
and Beverly

UNITED STATES DISTRICT COURT

DISTRICT OF ARIZONA

JOHN J. and VIRGINIA M. husband and wife, Plaintiffs, v. et al., Defendants.	No. CIV PHX WPC MARK MEMORANDUM IN SUPPORT OF MOTION TO COMPEL PRODUCTION OF DOCUMENTS

Preliminary Statement

On January 11, 1991, counsel for the plaintiffs in this action telephoned Mark Fairall and made notes of his conversation. Mr. does not recall the conversation. Counsel for the plaintiffs identified his notes of that conversation as a document being withheld from production to the defendants. On May 24, 1991, Mr. was named as a defendant in this lawsuit.

This motion seeks the production of any records concerning that call. As a defendant in this action, Mr. is entitled to know what plaintiffs' counsel contends was said in that telephone conference.

As set forth below, the document defendants requested is a party statement, discoverable as of right under Fed. R. Civ. P. 26(b)(3). Fairness dictates that a statement obtained from a party, before he had obtained counsel, should not gain protection under the work product doctrine. Furthermore, defendants seek only the factual content of this document, not the opinions or mental impressions, if any, of plaintiffs' attorney. Thus, even if these documents were protected by the work product doctrine, defendants have shown substantial need, and the inability to obtain the substantial equivalent, thereby entitling them to discovery under any theory.

Argument

I DEFENDANT MARK STATEMENT IS DISCOVERABLE AS A PARTY STATEMENT

A. A Party Has a Right to Discover His Own Statement

A party has an affirmative right to discover his own statement obtained by the opposing party. F.R.C.P. 26(b)(3). This rule is nondiscretionary--a party statement requested must be produced. Miles v. M/V Mississippi Queen, 753 F.2d 1349, 1351 (5th Cir. 1985). A showing of need and hardship is not required. F.R.C.P. 26(b)(3).

Rule 26(b)(3) defines "statement" broadly enough to cover the notes taken by Mr. here. Statement includes an "other recording or a transcription thereof, which is a substantially verbatim recital of an oral statement by the person making it and contemporaneously recorded."[1] F.R.C.P. 26(b)(3).

Statement "encompass[es] more than mere automatic reproductions of oral statements."[2] Palermo v. United States, 360 U.S. 343, 352 (1959). "Substantially verbatim" does not mean precisely verbatim. Phelps v. Commissioner, 62 T.C. 513, 517 (1974). The nonverbatim notes of an oral interview are discoverable as long as the notes attempt accurately to reflect what was said. Id.; Palermo, 360 U.S. at 352-53.

Mr. said he took one page of handwritten notes during a phone conversation with the defendant Mr. . Surely Mr. believes his notes purport to reflect what was said in the conversation because he says they were taken contemporaneously--therefore they are discoverable as of right under Rule 26(b)(3).

B. The Party Statement Exception Should Be Read Broadly and Defendant Mark s Statement Should Be Produced in the Interest of Fairness

It is undisputed that the notes reflect a conversation between plaintiffs' counsel and a defendant before he was represented by counsel. We do not contend (at least at this point) that the contact was improper. But to permit plaintiffs sole access to the only

[1] The definition of statement is "(A) a written statement signed or otherwise adopted or approved by the person making it, or (B) a stenographic, mechanical, electrical, or other recording, or a transcription thereof, which is a substantially verbatim recital of an oral statement by the person making it and contemporaneously recorded." F.R.C.P. 26(b)(3).

[2] This definition is adopted from the Jencks Act, 18 U.S.C. § 3500(e), and thus the caselaw interpreting it gives guidance in the discovery context.

apparent record of that conversation gives them an unfair advantage. E.g., 8 C. Wright & A. Miller, Federal Practice and Procedure § 2027 at 237 (2d ed. 1990) (In order to avoid giving "one side to a case an advantage if they are swift enough to deal with their potential opponent before he has retained counsel, conduct that is not permitted to them after an attorney has been retained by the opponent," the party statements rule must be read broadly).

The purpose of the rule is clear--to maintain fairness and prevent "trial by ambush." Miles, 753 F.2d at 1353; Advisory Committee Notes, 1970 Amendment to Rule 26(b)(3). A party statement is broadly defined in this context because it is admissible in evidence and could thus result in inequities:

> [o]rdinarily, a party gives a statement without insisting on a copy because he does not yet have a lawyer and does not understand the legal consequences of his actions. Thus, the statement is given at a time when he functions at a disadvantage. Discrepancies between his trial testimony and earlier statement may result from lapse of memory or ordinary inaccuracy; a written statement produced for the first time at trial may give such discrepancies a prominence which they do not deserve.

Advisory Committee Notes, 1970 Amendment to Rule 26(b)(3).

The purpose of the discovery rules is to give a party access to all admissible evidence. Hickman v. Taylor, 329 U.S. 495, 515 (1947) (Jackson, J., concurring). Yet, "[t]he lawyer whose client has given a statement to his opponent before retaining counsel has no way whatever to see what this evidence will be if production is denied." 8 C. Wright & A. Miller § 2027 at 235.

Courts have often required party statements to be produced on fairness grounds. See Straughan v. Barge MVL NO. 802, 291 F. Supp.

282, 285 (S.D. Tx. 1968) (requiring disclosure based on fairness and consistency with the purpose of the federal rules); New York Cent. R.R. v. Carr, 251 F.2d 433, 435 (4th Cir. 1957) (fairness requires that "any substantially contemporaneous declarations" made when unrepresented by counsel be disclosed); Phelps, 62 T.C. at 518 ("the ends of justice" would not be served by forcing those who made statements when unrepresented by counsel to go to trial without their attorneys having advance knowledge of substantive evidence).

We do not know what use plaintiffs intend to make of Mr. conversation with Mr. , and to permit plaintiffs unilateral access to the substance of the conversation would thwart the very purpose of the discovery rules, and would only encourage lawyers to use extrajudicial means to obtain statements from unwitting defendants.

II. THE STATEMENT IS DISCOVERABLE BECAUSE SUBSTANTIAL NEED AND UNDUE HARDSHIP CAN BE SHOWN HERE

Rule 26(b)(3) gives qualified immunity to documents prepared in anticipation of litigation by or for a party. Upon a showing of substantial need and undue hardship in obtaining the substantial equivalent, factual work product documents must be produced. F.R.C.P. 26(b)(3).

The purpose of the work product doctrine is to "prevent exploitation of a party's efforts in preparing for litigation." Admiral Ins. Co. v. United States Dist. Court for the Dist. of Arizona, 881 F.2d 1486, 1494 (9th Cir. 1989); United States v. 22.80 Acres of Land, 107 F.R.D. 20, 24 (N.D. Cal. 1985). The purpose is not to prevent access to facts or evidence underlying an opponent's case. See Hickman, 329 U.S. at 507, 511.

Substantial need and undue hardship exist here. Plaintiffs may attempt to use the notes for impeachment--or even as evidence--but in any event they have already guided their framing of the complaint and joinder of Mr. . And since Mr. does not even recall the conversation, Mr. cannot gain the substantial equivalent of Mr. s notes.

Thus, Mr. statement, obtained and recorded by plaintiffs' attorney Mr. clearly is discoverable under any theory. Although it should be produced under the party statement exception to the work product rule, even if this court were to find the document to be protected under the work product doctrine, it is discoverable based on need and hardship.

Conclusion

For the reasons set forth above, defendants' motion pursuant to Rules 37(a) and 34(b) of the Federal Rules of Civil Procedure to compel plaintiffs to produce this document should be granted, and defendants should be awarded the reasonable expenses incurred in bringing this motion.

December 6, 1991

. . .

. . .

. . .

. . .

. . .

"At-Will" Employee does Not Mean "When You Want" Harkins !!

STUDY GUIDE
CHAPTER NINETEEN

1. What are joint tortfeasors? (383)

2. What does it mean to be "jointly and severally" liable? (383)

(a) What is a concurrent tortfeasor? (383)

(1) Does the rule of joint liability apply to concurrent tortfeasors? (383)

(b) Does this rule mean that a plaintiff can recover several times for his/her injuries? (383)

(c) Under this rule can one defendant be held responsible for all of the damages even though there are several defendants? (383-384)

(d) Does this rule apply if the harm cannot be apportioned? (384)

(e) Does this rule apply if the plaintiff is killed? (384)

(f) Does this rule apply if the plaintiff's property is destroyed? (384)

3. What is the rule regarding liablity if the defendants act in concert but only one of the defendants actually causes the injury to the plaintiff? (384)

4. Why has joint and several liability been abolished in some states? (384)

5. How have some states limited this doctrine? (384)

6. How many times can a plaintiff satisfy a judgment? (384)

7. What does it mean when it is said that a defendant seeks contribution? (385)

(a) Did the early American courts allow contribution? (385)

(b) What is the status of the rule regarding contribution today? (385)

(1) Is contribution allowed for intentional tortfeasors? (385)

(c) What is the justification underlying contribution? (385)

(d) How are damages divided in the context of contribution in those states that have adopted comparative negligence? (385)

(e) What is the relationship between contribution and joint liability? (385)

(1) Can defendants seek contribution from a defendant who has raised a legitimate defense? (385)

8. What is a release? (385)

(a) What was the result under the common law if one defendant was released? (385)

(1) How did the parties get around this result? (385)

(b) What is the majority rule regarding the release of other tortfeasors when one tortfeasor is released? (385)

(c) How can a plaintiff preserve his/her right against the other tortfeasors when he/she releases one? (385-386)

9. What is the difference between a release and a covenant not to sue? (386)

(a) Why should plaintiffs be cautious about signing releases? (386)

10. What potential problem exists in the context of contribution when one defendant is released and the other defendants are not? (386)

(a) Under the traditional rule was contribution allowed? (386)

(1) What was the problem with this rule? (386)

(b) What two alternatives have been used to circumvent this problem? (387)

(1)

(2)

(c) What are the potential problems with these two solutions? (387)

(1)

(2)

11. What is a "Mary Carter" or "Gallagher" agreement? (391)

(a) Does the contracting defendant remain a party in the case and does he/she participate at trial? (381)

(b) How, then, does the defendant benefit by such an agreement? (391)

(c) What effect do these agreements have on the no-contribution rule? (391)

(d) Are these agreements permissible? (391)

(e) Can the existence of these agreements be brought to the attention of the trier of fact? (391)

(f) What is the up-side and down-side of these agreements? (391)

12. What is meant by saying that one party has indemnified another party? (392)

(a) Give an example of indemnification. Identify who the indemnitor and indemnitee are in your example. (392)

(b) What is the difference between indemnification and contribution? (392)

(c) What is the justification for indemnification? (392)

(d) Why might a manufacturer indemnify a retailer? (392)

(e) Why might a sheriff be indemnified even if he/she wrongfully seizes someone's property? (392)

(f) In what situation might a defendant be indemnified by the doctor who treated the plaintiff? (392)

(g) What is equitable indemnity? (393)

REVIEW QUESTIONS

1. Under what circumstances might defendants be jointly and severally liable and what are the implications of being jointly and severally liable?

2. When is a defendant entitled to contribution?

3. What problems arise with contribution when one defendant is released? How have the courts attempted to deal with this problem?

4. What is the difference between contribution and indemnification? When is indemnification appropriate?

5. Why do parties sometimes enter into "Mary Carter" or "Gallagher" agreements?

PUTTING IT INTO PRACTICE

Your client is one of several defendants in a professional negligence case. What are some things you might consider as a way of reducing the amount of damages for which your client will be personally responsible if he is found liable? Assume your client and the other defendants are joint tortfeasors.

KEY TERMS

Define the following:

Concurrent tortfeasors

Contribution

Covenant not to sue

Indemnification

Joint and several liability

Joint tortfeasor

Mary Carter agreement

Release

Satisfaction

The following page represents a simple medical authorization release form.

MEDICAL AUTHORIZATION RELEASE

TO WHOM IT MAY CONCERN:

Please be advised that my attorney, J. STANLEY EDWARDS, EDWARDS & EDWARDS, is hereby authorized to request, and to receive, all medical information which you may have in your possession concerning me.

You are hereby authorized to allow my attorney complete access to any and all of my medical records, including billing statements, which are or may later be in your possession or in any way reflect anything concerning me. I hereby waive, in favor of my attorney, any and all confidential relationships.

I hereby authorize the use of a photostatic copy of this Release as though it were an original.

____
Susan Smith

Date: January ___, 1992

Rest Stop, Next Exit
Next Stop 25 Mi.
Last Clear
CHANCE
ASSUMPTION
OF
RISK

STUDY GUIDE
CHAPTER TWENTY

1. What is the difference between first party and third party coverage? (396)

(a) Give an example of first party coverage. (396)

(b) Give an example of third party coverage. (396)

(c) Is automobile insurance an example of first party or third party coverage? Explain your answer. (397)

2. How does the 1943 New York Standard Policy relate to fire insurance? (399)

(a) Who decides whether a structure damaged by fire will be repaired, rebuilt or replaced? (399)

(b) What is one thing an insured must prove before he/she can recover under any fire policy? (399)

(c) Can the amount paid an insured ever exceed the fair market value or replacement cost of the property? (399)

3. What is the purpose of accident insurance? (399)

(a) How does a policy normally compensate an insured for injuries sustained? (399-400)

(1) Is any type of accidental injury covered? (400)

(b) How does accident insurance compare to health insurance? (400)

4. What is the purpose of health insurance? (400)

(a) Do most health insurance policies require a deductible? (400)

(b) What is a co-insurance limit? (400)

(1) When a co-insurance limit exists what is an insured responsible for paying? (400)

(c) Do most policies set a limit on the amount of damages for which the insurer will be held responsible? (400)

5. What is a pre-existing condition? (400)

(a) In what way are pre-existing conditions relevant to health insurance coverage? (400)

(b) What is an exclusion and how does it relate to pre-existing conditions? (400)

(c) How do the courts deal with an insured's failure to disclose a prior medical condition? (400-401)

6. What is the primary purpose of homeowners' insurance? (401)

(a) What is the difference between basic and extended coverage? (401)

(b) What is the minimum coverage required by most lenders? (401)

(c) What do most homeowners' policies typically exclude? (401)

(d) Is coverage generally provided for acts that occur at places other than the insured's residence? (401)

(e) Is an insured covered for injuries caused by the insured or one of the insured's family? (401)

(f) Are medical payments provided for under any homeowners' policies? (401)

7. What does liability insurance cover? (401)

(a) Does liability insurance cover illegal or intentional acts committed by the insured? (401)

8. What is the difference between single limit and split limits coverage? (401-402)

(a) Give an example of a single limit policy. (401)

(b) Give an example of a split limits policy. (402)

9. How does life insurance differ from other types of insurance? (402)

(a) Why are there so many varieties of life insurance? (402)

(b) What are the potential tax benefits of investing in life insurance? (402)

10. What are the characteristics of each of the following kinds of insurance?

(a) Ordinary life insurance (402)

(b) Term life insurance (402)

(c) Joint life insurance (402)

(d) Survivorship life insurance (403)

11. In what situations would one want to choose each of the following types of insurance?

(a) Ordinary life insurance (402)

(b) Term life insurance (402)

(c) Joint life insurance (402)

(d) Survivorship life insurance (403)

12. Why would one want to buy marine insurance? (403)

13. What is the difference between malpractice insurance and errors and omissions insurance? (403)

14. What has been done to malpractice insurance recently that lowers the amount of coverage available to claimants? (403)

15. What is the problem with product liability insurance? (404)

(a) What do many providers of product liability insurance require before issuing policies? (404)

16. What is the purpose of life insurance? (404)

(a) What are the two forms of property insurance and how do they differ? (404)

(1)

(2)

17. What is the purpose behind title insurance? (404)

(a) Does a problem in a title necessarily involve damages? (404)

(b) What are the three types of title insurance? (405)

(1)

(2)

(3)

(c) Which of these types of policies is generally more expensive? (405)

18. Why are state statutes particularly relevant to any discussions involving unemployment insurance? (405)

19. Can an employee sue his/her employer for negligence in addition to receiving benefits from worker's compensation?

(a) Is worker's compensation available even if the employee was at fault? (406)

20. What are two defenses an insurer can raise against an insured?

(a)

(b)

21. What are the potential consequences of an applicant making a material misrepresentation on an insurance application? (407)

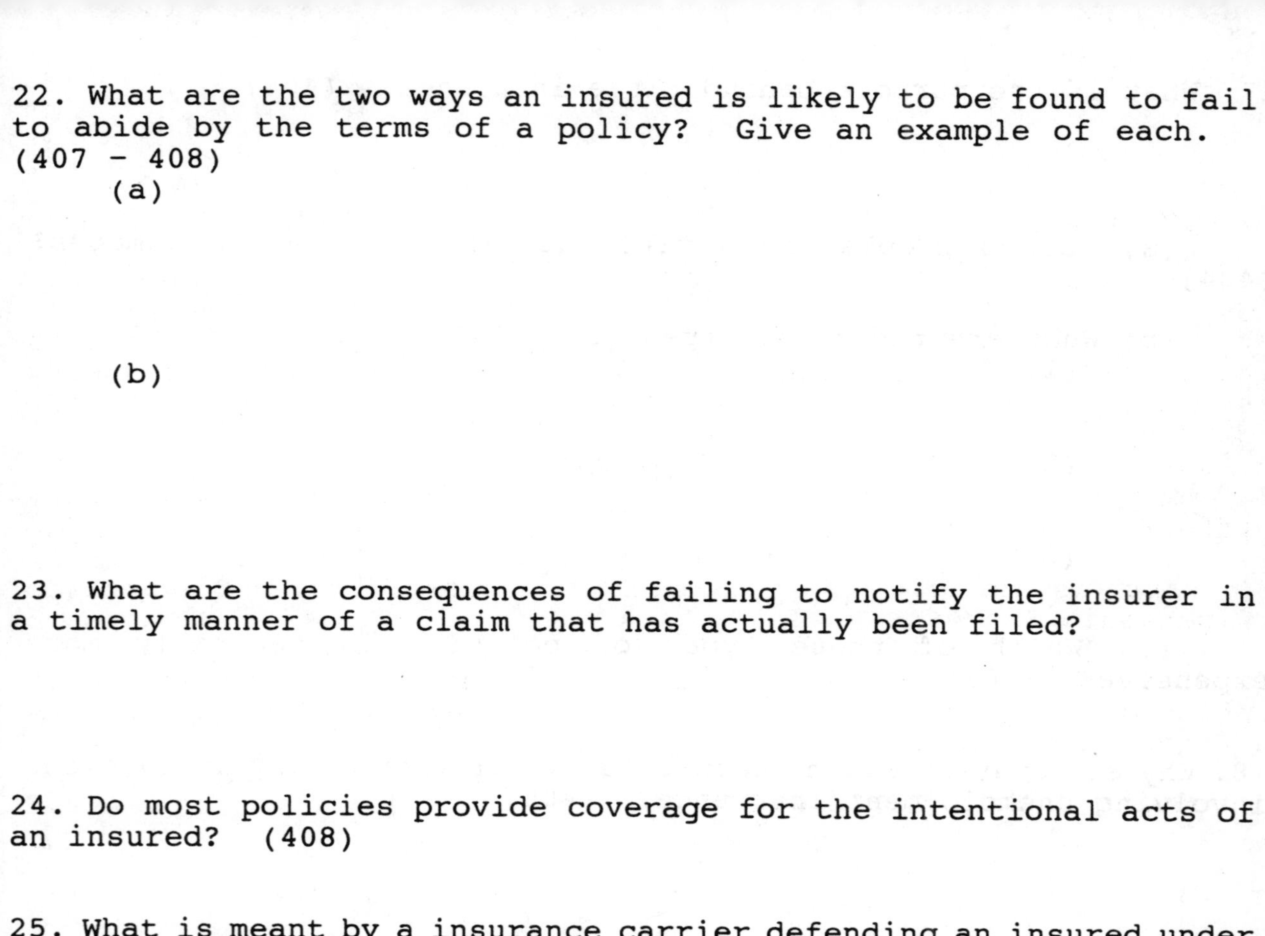

22. What are the two ways an insured is likely to be found to fail to abide by the terms of a policy? Give an example of each. (407 - 408)

(a)

(b)

23. What are the consequences of failing to notify the insurer in a timely manner of a claim that has actually been filed?

24. Do most policies provide coverage for the intentional acts of an insured? (408)

25. What is meant by a insurance carrier defending an insured under a reservation of rights? (408)

(a) May an insurer later withdraw after proceeding under a reservation of rights? (408)

26. Can an insurer ever be denied the right to assert a defense against an insured? (408)

(a) How are policy provisions that violate public policy treated by the courts? (408 - 409)

REVIEW QUESTIONS

1. Give examples of first party and third party coverage.

2. Give examples of single limit and split limits coverage.

3. Distinguish among the following: accident insurance, health insurance, homeowners' insurance, liability insurance, property insurance, malpractice insurance and errors and omissions insurance.

4. What are the four types of life insurance and how do they differ?

5. What is unique about unemployment insurance and worker's compensation?

6. What defenses can an insurer raise against its insured? What option does an insurer have while it is determining whether it has a right to deny coverage?

PUTTING IT INTO PRACTICE

A friend of yours owns a small business and has a family of four young children. She is thinking about purchasing insurance and wants to know what types of insurance would be best for her. Tell her the basic types of insurance that are available and the general provisions for each.

KEY TERMS

Define the following:

Actual cash value

ALTA policy

Basic coverage

Co-insurance limit

Extended coverage

First party coverage

Lender's policy

Loan value

Owner's policy

Pre-existing condition

Replacement cost policy

Reservation of rights

Single limit policy

Split limits policy

Third party coverage

The following pages are an example of a medical expenses worksheet.

LIST OF MEDICAL EXPENSES FOR
MARC ____
(As of February 5, 1991)

Name of Doctor Rendering Service	Date Claim Incurred	Date Claim Submitted	Amount
Humana Hospital Desert Valley	1-20-89	2-17-89	928.08
Anthony T. M.D.	1-24-89	3-20-89	100.00
Desert Valley Radiology	1-20-89	"	251.00
Blaine's United Drug	1-30-89	"	9.98
City of Phoenix EMS Trans. Service	1-20-89	"	160.00
Walgreens	2-1-89	"	6.69
Walgreens	2-13-89	"	6.69
Walgreens	2-13-89	"	5.49
Walgreens	2-2-89	3-24-89	4.89
Walgreens	3-5-89	"	6.79
Lynne B. D.O.	3-6/3-21-89	4-7-89	1,264.00
Lynne B. D.O.	3-30/4-3-89	4-18-89	304.00
Osco Drug	1-25-89	"	4.39
Eagle Medical Services	2-15/3-15-89	"	170.00
Lynne B. D.O.	5-25-89	7-5-89	132.00
Lynne B. D.O.	7-7-89	7-31-89	167.00
Lynne B. , D.O.	8-1/8-17-89	8-24-89	224.00
Lynne B. D.O.	10-31-89	11-10-89	75.00

Lynne B. . D.O.	11-2-89	"	177.00
Lynne B. , D.O.	11-3-89	"	105.00
Lynne B. , D.O.	11-6-89	"	65.00
Lynne B. , D.O.	11-8-89	11-22-89	45.00
Lynne B. , D.O.	11-8-89	"	65.00
Lynne B. , D.O.	11-13-89	"	30.00
Lynne B. D.O.	11-15-89	"	110.00
Lynne B. D.O.	11-17-21	11-28-89	80.00
Lynne B. , D.O.	11-21-89	"	65.00
Lynne B. D.O.	12-14-89	1-10-90	75.00
Lynne B. D.O.	1-5-90	1-12-90	132.00
Lynne B. , D.O.	1-8-90	"	90.00
Lynne B. D.O.	1-11-90	1-18-90	45.00
Lynne B. , D.O.	1-12-90	"	45.00
Lynne B. , D.O.	1-16-90	1-23-90	150.00
Lynne B. D.O.	1-18-90	"	45.00
Lynne B. D.O.	1-24-90	2-2-90	105.00
Lynne B. D.O.	1-25-90	"	60.00
Lynne B. D.O.	1-30-90	2-15-90	60.00
Walgreens	12-28-89	"	12.29
Lynne B. D.O.	4-3-90	4-11-90	45.00
Lynne B. D.O.	4-5/4-6-90	4-16-90	135.00
Lynne B. D.O.	4-18-90	4-27-90	135.00
Lynne B. D.O.	5-18-90	6-6-90	45.00
Lynne B. D.O.	5-23-90	"	189.00
Lynne B. D.O.	7-10-90	"	35.00

Lynne B. D.O.	7-10-90	"	35.00
Brad M.D.	9-13-90	10-4-90	3,789.00
Scottsdale Memorial Hospital - North	9-13-90	10-22-90	1,275.08
Scottsdale Memorial Hospital - North	9-13-90	11-5-90	52.00
Lynne B. D.O.	11-5-90	11-21-90	100.00
Walgreens Pharmacy (Brad M.D.)	9-13-90	12-5-90	20.89
Walgreens Pharmacy (Brad M.D.)	9-13-90	"	9.49
Walgreens Pharmacy (Brad M.D.)	9-14-90	"	9.19
Chiro. Clinic	1-25/5-25-89	1-4-91	2,530.00.
Brad R. M. D.	1-16-91	1-29-91	35.00
Desert Valley Radiology	1-18-90	2-5-91	36.00
	TOTAL:		13,856.94

Mandatory Insurance

Then

Now

STUDY GUIDE
CHAPTER TWENTY-ONE

1. What are two reasons underlying the extensive litigation of automobile insurance claims? (414)

(a)

(b)

2. What is "no fault" insurance? (414)

3. Give an example of "split limits" insurance. (415)

(a) How does "single limits" coverage differ from "split limits" coverage? (415)

4. What is an umbrella policy? (415)

(a) At what point does an umbrella carrier become liable? (415)

5. When will a court "reform" a policy? (415)

6. Define the term "subrogation." (416)

(a) For what types of insurance is subrogation allowed? (416)

(b) What does an insured have an obligation to do in a subrogation claim? (416)

7. What does medical payment coverage provide? (417)

(a) What is meant by primary coverage? (417)

(b) Whose coverage is primary if the insured is injured in someone else's vehicle? (417)

(1) What happens if the insured's medical expenses exceed the owner's limits? (417)

(c) Is there a time limit in which medical expenses must be incurred? (417)

(1) What happens if this time limit is exceeded? (417)

(d) Can an injured party recover twice for his/her medical expenses? (417)

(1) How does a "coordination of benefits" provision affect double recovery? (417)

(e) Do most medical payment plans have death benefits? (417)

8. What does comprehensive insurance cover? (417)

(a) What is the difference between reimbursement on the basis of actual cash value and reimbursement on the basis of replacement value?

(b) What do some policies require before allowing recovery for stolen property? (418)

(b) Is comprehensive required? (418)

9. What does collision insurance provide? (418)

(a) What happens if the responsible party is an uninsured motorist? (418)

10. What is the primary purpose of an emergency road service provision? (418)

(a) What other "accessory" coverages are available? (418)

(b) Why should care be taken in choosing "accessory" coverages? (418)

11. What is UM coverage? (419)

(a) Is UM coverage required? (419)

(b) Who sets the minimum limits and what are they usually? (419)

(c) Define "uninsured motorist." (419)

(d) Why is it important to have good UM coverage? (419)

(e) Are damages paid by an insurer reduced in proportion to the insured's negligence? (419)

(f) Can an insurer offset monies paid under a medical payment policy against the amount due an insured under his UM coverage? (419)

12. What would be the primary and secondary coverages in a case in which the insured is injured while driving a vehicle not specifically referred to in the policy? (419)

(a) At what point does the secondary coverage come into play? (419-420)

13. What happens if an insured, in addition to his UM coverage, has additional relevant coverage, which has a "coordination of benefits" provision? (420)

14. When is UIM coverage applicable? (420)

13. What is meant by the "stacking" of UM and UIM claims? (420)

(a) Can a responsible party be designated as uninsured and underinsured by the insured? (420)

14. What kinds of policies require arbitration in the event of a dispute? (420)

(a) How are arbiters selected? (421)

(b) In what cases is an arbitration award not binding? (421)

(1) What are the consequences if the award is not binding? (421)

15. Under what two conditions can an insurance contract be terminated? (421)

(a)

(b)

17. Must timely notice be given if an insured decides to terminate his/her policy? (421)

(a) How does mandatory insurance complicate termination? (421)

(b) What must an insurer do if it decides to terminate an insured's policy? (421)

(c) Is termination generally allowed for non-payment? (421)

(1) When does such termination become effective? (421)

(d) For what reason other than non-payment can an insurer terminate an insured's policy? (421)

REVIEW QUESTIONS

1. Distinguish the following types of coverage: liability, medical payment, comprehensive, collision, accessory, uninsured and underinsured.

2. What is the difference between primary and secondary coverage and when does secondary coverage come into play?

3. When is an umbrella policy applicable?

4. What are the subrogation rights of an insurer?

5. Under what circumstances is an insurer entitled to terminate an insured?

6. Describe the arbitration process used in resolving disputes over insurance coverage.

PUTTING IT INTO PRACTICE

A friend of yours is involved in an automobile accident resulting in extensive property damage and some personal injuries. She was driving her mother's car at the time. The other driver's insurance will not cover the full extent of the damages involved. What type of information should you suggest your friend have before going to see an attorney? What can you tell her in general about how she will most likely be able to recover for her losses?

KEY TERMS

Define the following:

Actual cash value

Comprehensive coverage

Collision coverage

Coordination of benefits provision

Primary coverage

Reformation of a policy

Replacement cost

Stacking of policies

UIM coverage

UM coverage

Secondary coverage

Subrogation

Umbrella policy

The following letter is a sample communication with an adjuster.

EDWARDS & EDWARDS

Attorneys at Law

J. Stanley Edwards

Linda L. Edwards

11000 North Scottsdale Road
Suite 135
Scottsdale, Arizona 85254
Phone: (602) 991-1938
Fax: (602) 991-2480

April 13, 1992

Ms. Dana W. Ladd
Claim Specialist
XYZ Mutual Automobile
Insurance Company
P. O. Box 1234
Phoenix, Arizona 85001-1234

Re: My Client/Your Insured: Susan Smith
Date of Accident: December 26, 1991
Your Claim No. 03-1300-540

Dear Ms. Ladd:

Thank you for your letter of February 19, 1992. You should be advised that I have forwarded you all records that I have received from Dr. Andrew Sweet. I am enclosing the Authorization to Provide Information which has been signed by Susan Smith. If you need a prognosis and maximum medical improvement date from Dr. Sweet, please contact Dr. Sweet directly. If he needs additional authorization forms in order to provide you with that information, I can assure you my client will cooperate with State Farm to ensure you receive the information you reasonably require. I should advise you, however, that any charges for this "special" information which you indicate you need will be the responsibility of XYZS Mutual.

It would appear that as of this date you have <u>not</u> reviewed and/or evaluated the medical bills previously submitted. I would suggest that you do so immediately. I <u>will not</u> tolerate any inordinate delay and unreasonable failure to process Mrs. Smith's reasonable medical expenses as her husband, Joseph Smith, was recently forced to endure. In that regard, I would refer you to A.R.S. §20-461 regarding our Unfair Claims Settlement Procedures

Act.

The last paragraph of your letter indicates that under certain circumstances some of Mrs. Smith's current or future charges might not be compensable under her medical payments coverage. To the extent that **<u>any</u>** of those charges you have received to date appear, in any way, to constitute anything other than reasonable expenses for necessary medical treatment for bodily injury caused by the accident, please advise me immediately. To the extent that any such questions may currently exist with respect to Mrs. Smith's treatment, you are, of course, entitled at your expense and at your discretion, to an independent medical examination.

I look forward to hearing from you regarding these matters at your earliest opportunity. If you have any questions concerning this matter, please do not hesitate to contact me at your convenience.

Very truly yours,

EDWARDS & EDWARDS

By J. Stanley Edwards
For the Firm

JSE/j
Encl.
cc: Mrs. Susan Smith

Well, I hope You Have Insurance!!

STUDY GUIDE
CHAPTER TWENTY-TWO

1. Why is bad faith considered an intentional tort? (428)

2. What are three ways bad faith can occur? (428)

(a)

(b)

(c)

3. What are adhesion contracts? (428-429)

(a) What reason have the courts used to justify scrutinizing insurance contracts more carefully than some other contracts? (429)

4. What reason did the courts give for interpreting insurance contracts in favor of the insured? (429)

5. What is the reasonable expectations doctrine? (429)

6. Why have the courts looked to remedies outside of contract law when insurers abused their discretion? (429)

7. What is the consequence of a court finding a fiduciary duty between an insurer and an insured? (429)

8. How did the tort of bad faith evolve? (428-430)

9. Is the question of bad faith a factual or legal question? (430)

10. What is the difference between a first party and third party claim? (430)

11. Can a bad faith claim also involve a breach of contract claim? (430)

(a) Can a bad faith claim exist in the absence of a breach of contract claim? (430)

(1) Give an example. (430)

12. Can an insurer sue an insured on the basis of bad faith? (430)

(a) What kinds of damages can be recovered on behalf of the insurer? (430)

13. How does a third party claim typically arise? (430-431)

14. What is an excess judgment? (431)

(a) What might an insured do after an excess judgment is entered? (431)

(1) What types of claims can an insured assign to an injured party? (431)

(2) What happens after the assignment is made? (431)

(3) Can an insured assign his/her rights to an injured party when the insurer defends the insured under a reservation of rights? (431)

15. Why is an insured to whom coverage is denied treated differently for purposes of bad faith claims than one who was defended under a reservation of rights? (431)

(a) What kind of agreement do the courts typically allow insureds who have been denied coverage to enter into with injured parties? (431)

(1) What can the injured party do once judgment is entered? (431)

(2) What can the injured party recover if the insurer denied coverage in bad faith? (431-432)

16. Why is the insured in a better position when a insurer defends under a reservation of rights than when coverage is denied outright? (432)

(a) What kind of agreement may an insured enter into under these circumstances? (432)

(1) Is such an agreement a violation of the cooperation clause found in most insurance contracts? (432)

(2) Must the insured advise the insurer of any such agreement? (432)

(b) How may an injured party resolve a reservation of rights case? (432)

(c) How does suit in a reservation of rights case differ from suit in a denial of coverage case? (432)

(1) What must the jury be told in a reservation of rights case? (432)

(2) What options does a jury have after hearing the evidence? (432)

17. How can bad faith occur even when an insurer acknowledges coverage and provides a complete defense? (432-433)

(a) Why are insureds particularly concerned about areas of liability where the damages are very large? (433)

(b) Why might an insured want to assign his/her rights to a bad faith claim to the injured party if the bad faith claim was based on the carrier's failure to settle a claim within policy limits? (433)

(c) Why do most courts prohibit an insured who an insurer has refused to settle within policy limits from entering into an agreement with an injured party before an excess judgment is entered? (433)

18. On what four factors are damages in third party cases based? (433)

(a)

(b)

(c)

(d)

19. What are punitive damages based on in a third party claim? (434)

20. What might a carrier do that could result in a first party bad faith claim? (434)

(a) Can an insurer use information obtained after filing a bad faith claim to justify its prior actions? (434)

21. How do the factors considered in damages awarded in third party claims differ from those awarded in first party claims? (433-434)

(a) What do unpaid benefits include? (434)

(b) Is it ever possible for an insured to recover for damages resulting from inability to pay bills if such inability arguably stems from the insurer's bad faith? (435)

22. For what reasons might an insured be exposed to less risk in a first party case than in a third party case? (435)

23. Describe two standards used by the courts in first party bad faith claims to determine whether bad faith has occurred.

(a)

(b)

24. What is the "equal consideration" test? (435)

(a) In what types of cases is this test used? (435)

(b) How does this test compare to the "fairly debatable" test? (435)

(c) What are some of the factors included in this test? (441)

(1)

(2)

(3)

(4)

(d) Must all eight factors be met to satisfy the requirements of this test? (441)

25. What is a declaratory judgment action? (441)

(a) How are declaratory judgment actions used offensively? (441)

(b) How are such actions used defensively? (442)

26. What is a first party characteristic of UM and UIM claims? (442)

(a) What is a third party characteristic of UM and UIM claims? (442)

(b) Do most courts view UM and UIM claims as first party or third party claims? (442)

27. How are disputes involving damages resolved in UM and UIM cases? (442)

(a) How are disputes involving coverage resolved? (442)

28. Do UM and UIM carriers have an adverse relationship with their insureds? (442)

REVIEW QUESTIONS

1. Describe how the tort of bad faith came into existence.

2. What are the differences between first party and third party claims? In what way do UM and UIM claims exhibit characteristics of both?

3. What are the three ways that third party claims can arise and how are each of them resolved?

4. What standards do the courts use in determining whether an insurer's actions constitute bad faith?

PUTTING IT INTO PRACTICE

A friend of yours was involved in an automobile accident a year ago. The insurance carrier of the person driving the vehicle that rear-ended her is dragging its heels and your friend is beginning to wonder if the carrier is going to deny coverage. Tell your friend about the potential bad faith claim she might have against the carrier and the procedures that would be involved in resolving such a claim.

KEY TERMS

Define the following terms:

Adhesion contract

Declaratory judgment

Excess judgment

First party claim

Third party claim

The attached pages represent a sample settlement demand letter and a general release that is usually a requirement for entering into a settlement.

EDWARDS & EDWARDS

Attorneys at Law

J. Stanley Edwards

Linda L. Edwards

11000 North Scottsdale Road
Suite No. 135
Scottsdale, Arizona 85254
Phone: (602) 991-1938
Fax: (602) 991-2480

April 8, 1992

Ms. Marianne Marane
Claim Specialist
XYZ Mutual Automobile
Insurance Company
P. O. Box 1234
Phoenix, Arizona 85001-1234

Re: My Client: Susan Smith
Your Insured: Michael Jones
Date of Accident: December 26, 1991
Your Claim No. 03-1368-439

Dear Ms. Marane:

Please be advised that my client is no longer treating with either Dr. Sweet or her prescribed physical therapist, Steven E. Kash. It appears that Mrs. Smith's medical condition has stabilized to the point that future medical treatment and/or physical therapy would be of no further help to her.

After her accident of December 26, 1991, Mrs. Smith was first seen at Humane Hospital, emergency room and released. When additional problems surfaced, she was seen two days later at the same place and on December 30, 1991, began seeing Dr. Sweet who treated her as well as referred her for physical therapy with Steven E. Kash. Mrs. Smith treated with Mr. Kash on 20 separate occasions and with Dr. Sweet on three separate occasions. Mrs. Smith was also unable to return to work for two days after the accident and lost 16 hours of wage income at her hourly rate of $8.70 for a total of $139.20. Mrs. Smith was also off work for at least an additional eight hours when she was undergoing treatment but made arrangements to make up for the time at work. There are no documents to verify the additional hours she worked due to the accident in order to maintain her standard work week.

Although it does not appear that Mrs. Smith suffered any

permanent injuries as a result of the accident and that her condition has stabilized, she still occasionally suffers exacerbations of her condition which results in pain in her neck, shoulders and upper back as well as occasional headaches. These symptoms are consistent with the diagnosis of her condition made by Dr. Sweet wherein he opined that Mrs. Smith was suffering from a cervical and thoracic strain along with paresthesia in her left arm. Mrs. Smith's recovery was, of course, enhanced by her faithful adherence to the regimen prescribed by Dr. Sweet and Mr. Kash. I am aware of the minimal property damage that was caused to the Smith vehicle. I am sure you recognize, however, that the dropping of a steel box may not damage the box but would certainly break any eggs inside of it.

In any event, my client has authorized me to accept the sum of $7,500.00 as and for full and complete settlement of her claim against your insured. Resolution of this matter will save both parties the costs of arbitration in the Superior Court and eventual additional expenses should any decision be appealed. In light of Mrs. Smith's medical expenses, lost wages and pain and suffering and general inconvenience, we believe that her proposal is a most reasonable one and is not meant to be a starting point for "Nogales" negotiations.

I look forward to receipt of your Company's draft in the amount of $7,500.00, made payable to my client and myself, together with appropriate release documents at your earliest opportunity. If you have any questions concerning this matter, please do not hesitate to contact me at your convenience.

Very truly yours,

EDWARDS & EDWARDS

By J. Stanley Edwards
For the Firm

JSE/j
cc: Mrs. Susan Smith

GENERAL RELEASE

KNOW ALL MEN BY THESE PRESENTS:

For and in consideration of the sum of paid by Insurance Company, the undersigned Marc A. ______ hereby releases and forever discharges Insurance Company and Bernadette M. and all other potential tortfeasors, their firms, agents, servants or employees, and all other persons, firms and corporations, from any and all claims, demands, actions and causes of action, and any liability whatsoever, on account of or in any manner arising or to arise out of the personal injury and/or property loss by Marc A. Kosuda which occurred on or about January 20, 1989, which incident is the subject matter of that certain cause of action more particularly set forth in Cause No. CV , styled as Marc A. vs. Bernadette M. , said cause of action filed in the Superior Court of Maricopa County, State of Arizona, which claims are contemporaneously herewith dismissed with prejudice.

The execution of this instrument by the undersigned releases all claims, demands and causes of action of any kind whatsoever in connection with the above-named occurrence, including any and all injury and damages, even though presently unsuspected and unknown.

THIS RELEASE IS INTENDED TO AND DOES COVER ALL DAMAGES, WHETHER KNOWN TO THE PARTIES AT THE TIME OF THE EXECUTION OF THIS AGREEMENT OR NOT, WHICH HAVE RESULTED OR MAY HEREAFTER RESULT, OR WHICH MAY HEREAFTER BE DISCOVERED, AND WHICH MAY HAVE BEEN CAUSED OR MAY BE CLAIMED TO HAVE BEEN CAUSED BY THE SAID INCIDENT.

The parties to this instrument recognize that THE UNDERSIGNED MAY HAVE SUSTAINED DAMAGES WHICH ARE UNKNOWN at the time of the execution hereof, and INTEND BY THE EXECUTION OF THIS INSTRUMENT TO RELEASE ANY CLAIM FOR SUCH UNKNOWN DAMAGES. It is further understood and agreed that part of the consideration set forth above paid to the undersigned is to compensate the undersigned for unknown damages that may be discovered in the future.

The undersigned hereby warrants that out of the proceeds paid herein the undersigned will satisfy any and all unpaid or unsatisfied liens, and that the undersigned will indemnify and hold harmless Insurance Company and Bernadette M. and all other potential tortfeasors, their firms, agents, servants or employees, and all other persons, firms and corporations, from any liability whatsoever, including but not limited to costs, attorneys' fees or judgments which might arise from an unpaid or unsatisfied lien or any nature which might apply to the proceeds paid herein or otherwise resulting from the involvement in the aforesaid incident.

It is understood and agreed that the payment of this sum is not to be construed as an admission of liability on the part of Insurance Company and Bernadette M. and any and all other potential tortfeasors, liability therefore being expressly denied, but is in compromise and settlement of a disputed claim.

IN WITNESS WHEREOF, Marc A. has hereunto set his hand this 10th day of April, 1992.

MARC A.

WITNESSED AND APPROVED:

Stanley Edwards. Attorney For Marc A.

STATE OF ARIZONA)
) ss.
County of Maricopa)

On this, the 10th day of April, 1992, before me, the undersigned Notary Public, appeared Marc A. to me known to be the person who executed the foregoing instrument, and acknowledged that he executed the same as and for his free act and deed for the purposes therein contained.

WITNESS my hand and official seal.

Notary Public

My Commission Expires: